East Asia in Transition:
Challenges for the Trilateral Countries

A Task Force Report to
The Trilateral Commission

Authors: RICHARD C. HOLBROOKE
Managing Director, Shearson Lehman Hutton Inc.;
former U.S. Assistant Secretary of State for
East Asian and Pacific Affairs

RODERICK MACFARQUHAR
Professor of Government and Director, Fairbank
Center for East Asian Research, Harvard University;
former Member of Parliament, United Kingdom

KAZUO NUKAZAWA
Managing Director, Keidanren (Japan Federation of
Economic Organizations)

Associate Author: EVELYN COLBERT
Professorial Lecturer, School of Advanced International Studies, Johns Hopkins University;
former U.S. Deputy Assistant Secretary of State for
East Asian and Pacific Affairs

Library of Congress Cataloging-in-Publication Data

East Asia in Transition: Challenges for the Trilateral Countries:
  a report to the Trilateral Commission/Richard Holbrooke ...
[et al.].
          p. cm. -- (The Triangle papers ; 35)
ISBN 0-930503-04-X : $6.00
1. East-Asia--Politics and government. 2. East Asia--Economic
conditions. 3. East Asia--Foreign relations. I. Holbrooke, Richard C.
II. Trilateral Commission. III. Series.
DS518.1.E27 1988
320.95--dc19

                                                        88-16012
                                                        CIP

Manufactured in the United States of America

THE TRILATERAL COMMISSION

<table>
<tr><td>345 East 46th Street
New York, NY 10017</td><td>c/o Japan Center for
International Exchange
4-9-17 Minami-Azabu
Minato-ku
Tokyo, Japan</td><td>35, avenue de Friedland
75008 Paris, France</td></tr>
</table>

The Authors

RICHARD C. HOLBROOKE is a Managing Director at Shearson Lehman Hutton Inc. During the Carter Administration, he was Assistant Secretary of State for East Asian and Pacific Affairs. Educated at Brown University (A.B., 1962) and Princeton's Woodrow Wilson School, Mr. Holbrooke joined the U.S. Foreign Service in 1962. His ten years in the Foreign Service included service in Vietnam, on the White House Staff under President Johnson, at the 1968-69 Paris peace talks with the North Vietnamese, and as Peace Corps Director in Morocco. He was an author of one volume of *The Pentagon Papers*. In 1972-77, he was Editor of *Foreign Policy*. Mr. Holbrooke is a frequent contributor to *The Wall Street Journal*, *Newsweek*, *Foreign Affairs*, *The New York Times* and other publications.

RODERICK MACFARQUHAR is Professor of Government and Director of the John King Fairbank Center for East Asian Research at Harvard University. Educated at Oxford, Harvard, and London (Ph.D.) Universities, Dr. MacFarquhar's career has spanned journalism, politics and scholarly research. In journalism, he was a correspondent for the *Daily Telegraph* in 1955-61, and worked with the BBC (TV and World Service Radio) at three different periods in subsequent years. In politics, he was a Labour Member of Parliament in 1974-79, and later fought the 1983 general election for the Social Democratic Party. Before joining the Harvard faculty in 1984, he had periods at Columbia University (1969), the Royal Institute of International Affairs (1971-74), the Woodrow Wilson Center of the Smithsonian Institution (1980-81), and as a Leverhulme Research Fellow in the United Kingdom (1980-84). He was the editor of the *China Quarterly* in 1959-68. Among his many publications is a multi-volume work on the origins of China's Cultural Revolution.

KAZUO NUKAZAWA is Managing Director of the Keidanren (Japan Federation of Economic Organizations) in charge of international affairs. He studied at Hitotsubashi University (B.A. in Economics) and joined the Keidanren upon graduating in 1959. In 1964-65, he studied the competition policies of various European countries as a United Nations Fellow at the London School of Economics. He served as Consultant to the U.S.-Japan Trade Council (presently the Japan Economic Institute of America) in Washington, D.C., in 1968-71, and was a Visiting Research Fellow at the Rockefeller Foundation in 1978-79. Before becoming a Managing Director of Keidanren in 1988, Mr. Nukazawa was Director of the International Economic Affairs Department in 1985-88, and Director of the Financial Affairs Department in1982-85.

Evelyn Colbert (Associate Author) is a Professorial Lecturer at the Reischauer Institute of the School of Advanced International Studies of Johns Hopkins University. Educated at Barnard College and Columbia University (Ph.D., 1947), Dr. Colbert has had a long and distinguished career in U.S. government service dealing with East Asia—first in the Office of Strategic Services (1943-46) and then in the Department of State. In 1974-77, Mrs. Colbert was National Intelligence Officer for East Asia and the Pacific in the Office of the Director of Central Intelligence. She then returned to the State Department and, from April 1978 until her retirement in July 1980, was Deputy Assistant Secretary for East Asian and Pacific Affairs. She is the author of three books and numerous articles and papers, of which the most recent concern U.S. policy in Southeast Asia and U.S. military bases in the Philippines.

The Trilateral Process

The report which follows is the joint responsibility of its authors. Although only the authors are responsible for the analysis and conclusions, they have been aided in their work by many others. The persons consulted spoke for themselves as individuals and not as representatives of any institutions with which they are associated. Those consulted or otherwise assisting in the development of the report include the following:

Morton I. Abramowitz, *U.S. Assistant Secretary of State for Intelligence and Research*

Donald Anderson, *Member of British Parliament*

Arbinant Na Ranong, *Minister-Counsellor, Embassy of Thailand to the United States*

Tatsuo Arima, *Director-General, North American Bureau, Japanese Ministry of Foreign Affairs*

Michael Armacost, *U.S. Undersecretary of State*

Raymond-Max Aubert, *Director of the Cabinet of the French Minister of the Overseas Territories and Départements (DOM/TOM), Paris*

Giovanni Auletta Armenise, *Chairman, Banca Nazionale dell'Agricoltura, Rome*

Didier Bariani, *Secretary of State, Ministry of Foreign Affairs, Paris*

A. Doak Barnett, *George and Sadie Hyman Professor of Chinese Studies, School of Advanced International Studies, Johns Hopkins University*

Piero Bassetti, *Chairman of the Federation of Italian Chambers of Commerce*

Philippe Baude, *Former Ambassador, State Secretariat for the South Pacific, Paris*

Stephen Bosworth, *President, U.S.-Japan Foundation; former U.S. Ambassador to the Philippines*

Giovanni Bressi, *President, Centro Studi e Documentazione Internazionali (CESDI), Turin*

Brian Bridges, *Royal Institute for International Affairs, London*

Paolo Beonio Brocchieri, *Professor, Department of Politics, University of Pavia, Italy*

Hervé de Carmoy, *Administrator, Société Générale de Belgique, Brussels and Paris*

Lord Carrington, *Former Secretary General, NATO*

Umberto Colombo, *Chairman, National Committee for Nuclear Energy, Rome*

Alessandro Corneli, *Professor, Department of Politics, Libera Università Internazionale di Studi Sociali (LUISS), Rome*

Sir Robert Crichton-Brown, *Chairman, Rothmans International, London*

Viscount Etienne Davignon, *Former Vice President, Commission of the European Communities; Member of the Board of Directors, Société Générale de Belgique, Brussels*

Guido Declercq, *Chairman, Investco, Brussels*

Jean Deflassieux, *Chairman, Banque pour le Développement des Echanges Internationaux; Honorary Chairman, Crédit Lyonnais, Paris*

Hervé Dejean de La Batie, *Policy Planning Staff, Ministry of Foreign Affairs, Paris*

Paul Delouvrier, *Former Chairman, Public Authority for the Development of the Parc de la Villette; former Chairman, French Electricity Board, Paris*

Paul Dimond, *China Desk, Foreign and Commonwealth Office, London*

Jean-Yves Domenach, *Head, Centre d'Etudes et de Recherches Internationales (CERI), Fondation Nationale des Sciences Politiques, Paris*

Michael Donnelly, *Director, Joint Centre for Asia Pacific Studies, University of Toronto and York University; Professor of Political Science, University of Toronto*

Irène Dupoux-Couturier, *President, Centre de Formation aux Réalités Internationales (CEFRI), Paris*

Jacques Edin, *French Institute for International Relations (IFRI), Paris*

Christopher Elston, *Senior Advisor Far East, Bank of England, London*

René Foch, *President, Télénorma France*

Benedetto Francese, *Political Department, Italian Ministry of Foreign Affairs, Rome*

Andrew V. Frankel, *Assistant North American Director, Trilateral Commission*

Hiroshi Fukuda, *Deputy Director-General of the Treaties Bureau, Japanese Ministry of Foreign Affairs*

Pieter de Geus, *Deputy Chairman, Board of Management, Netherlands Organization for Applied Scientific Research (TNO), The Hague; former Dutch Minister of Defense*

François Godement, *French Institute for International Relations (IFRI), Paris*

Jacques Groothaert, *Chairman of the Board, Société Générale de Banque, Belgium; Honorary Ambassador of Belgium*

Kate Grosser, *Royal Institute for International Affairs, London*

Harry Harding, *Senior Fellow, Foreign Policy Studies, Brookings Institution*

Sir William Harding, *Director, Lloyds Merchant Bank, London; former British Ambassador*

Charles B. Heck, *North American Director, Trilateral Commission*

Father Bryan Hehir, *Secretary, Department of Social Development & World Peace, U.S. Catholic Conference*

Stéphane Hessel, *Ambassadeur de France; former Assistant Administrator, UNDP; former Permanent Representative at the United Nations, Geneva*

Brigadier Kenneth Hunt, *International Institute for Strategic Studies, London*

Dennis Ignatius, *Counsellor, Embassy of Malaysia to the United States*

L. Oakley Johnson, *Vice President, International Corporate Affairs, American International Group, Washington, D.C.*

Gérard Julienne, *Deputy Director, Asia Department, Ministry of Foreign Affairs, Paris*

Henry J. Kenny, *Professional Staff Member, U.S. Senate Committee on Foreign Relations*

K.W. Kim, *Ambassador of the Republic of South Korea to the United States*

Tommy T.B. Koh, *Ambassador of Singapore to the United States*

Rodolphe de Koninck, *Professor, Department of Geography, Laval University, Canada*

Jean-Pierre Lafon, *Advisor on International Affairs to the French Prime Minister, Paris*

Peter Lyons, *Institute of Commonwealth Studies, London*

Kunihiko Makita, *Royal Institute for International Affairs, London, and Japanese Ministry of Foreign Affairs*

Claude Martin, *Director, Asia Department, Ministry of Foreign Affairs, Paris*

Robin McLaren, *Assistant Undersecretary of State (Far East), Foreign and Commonwealth Office, London*

Francis J. McNeil, *former Acting U.S. Deputy Assistant Secretary of State for East Asian and Pacific Affairs; former U.S. Ambassador to Costa Rica*

Wolf Mendl, *Professor, Kings College, University of London*

Cesare Merlini, *Chairman, Institute for International Affairs, Rome*

Jonathan Mirsky, The Observer, *London*

Corrado Molteni, *Associated Professor, Institute of Socio-Economic Studies for East Asia (ISESAO), Bocconi University, Milan*

Heinrich von Moltke, *Deputy Director-General, Internal Market and Industrial Affairs Directorate, Commission of the European Communities, Brussels*

Philippe Moreau-Defarges, *French Institute for International Relations (IFRI), Paris*

Charles Morrison, *Special Assistant to the President, East-West Center, Honolulu; Senior Research Associate, Japan Center for International Exchange, Tokyo*

Saji bin Mudin, *Chargé d'Affaires, Embassy of Brunei to the United States* viii

Karl-Heinz Narjes, *Vice President, Commission of the European Communities, Brussels*

Martin Nègre, *Vice President, Alsthom-Atlantique, Paris*

Laura Newby, *Royal Institute for International Affairs, London*

Makito Noda, *Program Officer, Japan Center for International Exchange, Tokyo*

Michael Oborne, *Assistant to the Deputy Secretary General, OECD, Paris*

Saburo Okita, *Chairman of the Institute for Domestic and International Policy Studies, Tokyo; former Japanese Minister for Foreign Affairs*

Georges Ordonnaud, *President, Institut du Pacifique, Paris*

Egidio Ortona, *Honorary Chairman, Honeywell Bull Italia; former Italian Ambassador to the United States*

Hisashi Owada, *Ambassador of Japan to the OECD*

Sir Michael Palliser, *Deputy Chairman, Midland Bank; Chairman of the Council, IISS ; former Permanent Under-Secretary of State, Foreign and Commonwealth Office, London*

Michel Paoletti, *Director of Cabinet of State Secretary for the South Pacific, Paris*

Park Yung-Chul, *Professor of Economics, Korea University; former Senior Secretary to the President for Economic Affairs, Republic of Korea*

Maynard Parker, *Editor*, Newsweek

Emmanuel Pelaez, *Ambassador of the Republic of the Philippines to the United States*

Jacques Pelletier, *Director, Banque Indosuez, Paris*

Giuseppe Piovano, *Deputy Chairman, Oto Melara, Rome; former Secretary General of the Italian Ministry of Defense*

Edgar Pisani, *Advisor to the President of the Republic, Paris; former Minister; former Member of the Commission of the European Communities*

Jean-Claude Pomonti, Le Monde, *Paris*

Pu Shan, *Director, Institute of World Economics and Politics, Chinese Academy of Social Sciences, Beijing*

Paul Révay, *European Director, Trilateral Commission*

John Roper, *Editor*, International Affairs, *Royal Institute for International Affairs, London; former Member of British Parliament*

François de Rose, *Ambassadeur de France; former Permanent Representative to NATO*

Stanley Roth, *Director of Asian & Pacific Affairs, Office of Congressman Stephen J. Solarz; Staff Director, Asian and Pacific Affairs Subcommittee, House Foreign Affairs Committee*

J. Stapleton Roy, *U.S. Deputy Assistant Secretary of State for East Asian and Pacific Affairs*

Seizaburo Sato, *Professor of Political Science, University of Tokyo*

Yukio Sato, *Assistant Vice-Minister for Parliamentary Affairs, Japanese Ministry of Foreign Affairs*

Robert A. Scalapino, *Robson Research Professor of Government and Director, Institute for East Asian Studies, University of California at Berkeley*

Masahide Shibusawa, *Director, East-West Seminar, Tokyo*

Peter Shore, *Member of British Parliament*

Stefano Silvestri, *Director, Institute for International Affairs, Rome*

Henri Simonet, *Member of Belgian Parliament*

John Smith, *Member of British Parliament; Shadow Chancellor of the Exchequer*

Soesilo Soedarman, *Ambassador of the Republic of Indonesia to the United States*

André de Staercke, *Honorary Ambassador of Belgium; former Permanent Representative to NATO*

Richard H. Solomon, *Director, Policy Planning Staff, U.S. Department of State*

Helmut Sonnenfeldt, *Guest Scholar, Brookings Institution; former Counselor, U.S. State Department*

John Swire, *Chairman, John Swire & Sons Group of Companies, London*

Sir Peter Tapsell, *Member of British Parliament; former Frontbench Spokesman on both Finance and Foreign Affairs*

Geoffrey Taylor, *Chairman, Daiwa Europe Finance; former Chairman, Midland Bank, London*

Niels Thygesen, *Professor of Economics, Economics Institute, Copenhagen University*

Ernesto Vellano, *Director, FIAT, Turin; Secretary of Italian Group of Trilateral Commission*

Alain Vernay, Le Figaro, *Paris*

Paolo Battino Vittorelli, *Former Member of Italian Parliament; Chairman, Istituto Studi e Ricerche Difesa; Head of Defense Department of Italian Socialist Party*

Kenneth Walker, *Research Department, Foreign and Commonwealth Office, London*

J.H. Warren, *Principal Trade Policy Advisor, Government of Quebec; former Canadian Ambassador to the United States*

Robin Webster, *Assistant Advisor Japan, Bank of England, London*

Tadashi Yamamoto, *Japanese Director, Trilateral Commission*

Donald Zagoria, *Professor of Political Science, Hunter College, City University of New York*

SCHEDULE OF TASK FORCE ACTIVITIES:

March 22, 1987 — Holbrooke, MacFarquhar and Yamamoto meet in San Francisco, in wings of Trilateral Commission plenary meeting, to discuss broad thrust of report.

May 12 — Holbrooke prepares brief description of report.

September 20 — Nukazawa submits outline for economics chapter.

October 1 — Holbrooke, MacFarquhar and Colbert meet in New York.

October 23-24 — Holbrooke, MacFarquhar and Nukazawa meet in Munich and discuss report with European members assembled for regional meeting.

December 1 — Nukazawa submits elements of economics chapter.

December 7 — Colbert submits outline of introduction and political evolution chapter.

December 9 — Holbrooke, Nukazawa and Colbert meet in New York.

January 1988 — First drafts completed of Introduction and Chapters I and II.

January 11 — MacFarquhar meets with British members and experts in London. Holbrooke and Colbert meet with ASEAN country representatives in Washington, D.C.

January 12 — MacFarquhar meets in Brussels with Belgian members and experts, and with leading EC and NATO officials.

January 13 — MacFarquhar meets with Italian members and experts in Rome.

January 14 — MacFarquhar meets with French members and experts in Paris.

January 16-18 — Holbrooke, MacFarquhar, Nukazawa and Colbert meet in Tokyo and hold consultations with Japanese experts.

February — Revised draft prepared including Introduction and Chapters I, II and III.

February 11 — Holbrooke, MacFarquhar, Nukazawa and Colbert meet in Washington, D.C., and discuss report with North American experts.

March 20 — Holbrooke completes draft of Chapter IV.

March 28 — Full draft completed and circulated to Trilateral Commission members.

April 10 — Draft report discussed in Trilateral Commission plenary meeting in Tokyo.

June — Final revisions completed.

Table of Contents

* * *

INTRODUCTION

Just as the mid-'60s marked the beginnings of a period of extraordinary growth and development along the East Asian rim of the Pacific, so in the late '80s new challenges confront the region—especially the developing countries of which it is still largely composed.[1] How these challenges are met will be of momentous consequence, not only to the developing countries of East Asia but also to the broader international system of which the Trilateral countries have been the principal custodians. The stability and prosperity of the region are of obvious importance to those Trilateral countries that are themselves Pacific nations—Japan, the United States and Canada. The stake of Western Europe is also large, perhaps more so than is yet recognized. In an interdependent global economy, the repercussions of the policies and economic health of such a populous and dynamic region are of major European concern. Even strategic interests can no longer be contained within separate geographic boxes labelled "Atlantic" and "Pacific." East Asian contributions to stability and deterrence are thus of significant importance to Western Europe.[2]

Looking back, it is easy to see that the foundations for the now widely anticipated "Pacific Century" were laid in the mid-'60s. Japan's economic miracle, already well underway, was fueling growth elsewhere in the region. The opportunities provided by an open and favorable global market were being effectively grasped by non-Communist East Asian countries. Adopting pragmatic market-oriented policies and guided by the conviction that the remedy for domestic turmoil lay in economic development and modernization, these countries achieved and maintained rates of growth unequalled elsewhere in the Third World—growth that was reflected in improved standards of living for their people.

---

[1] These countries include the People's Republic of China, North and South Korea, Hong Kong and Taiwan, the six ASEAN countries, the three Indochina countries, and Burma. Japan is, of course, a Trilateral country and a key country in the region. For purposes of this report, we have largely excluded the Pacific Islands, where the main problems—and their scale—are different. Australia and New Zealand are important countries in the broader region, but we have chosen not to focus on them in this report. The political evolution issues that are important in so much of developing East Asia are settled in Australia and New Zealand. Nor do Australia and New Zealand present the same sort of adaptation challenge to global economic arrangements and the Trilateral countries.

[2] See Masashi Nishihara, *East Asian Security and the Trilateral Countries*, A Report to the Trilateral Commission (New York: NYU Press, 1985).

TABLE 1
Population of East Asian Countries
1986, with Trilateral and Oceania comparisons
(millions of persons)

Japan	121.3	*Japan*	*121.3*
		EC	*322.8*
China	1,054.8	*USA*	*241.1*
		Canada	*25.6*
Northeast Asian NICs			
South Korea	41.6	*FRG*	*60.9*
Taiwan	19.4	*Italy*	*57.2*
Hong Kong	5.5	*UK*	*56.6*
		France	*55.4*
ASEAN		*Spain*	*38.9*
Indonesia	165.4	*Netherlands*	*14.5*
Philippines	56.0	*Portugal*	*10.3*
Thailand	52.6	*Belgium*	*9.9*
Malaysia	15.9	*Denmark*	*5.1*
Singapore	2.6	*Norway*	*4.2*
Brunei	0.2	*Ireland*	*3.6*
		Luxembourg	*0.4*
Indochina			
Vietnam	63.3		
Kampuchea	n.a.		
Laos	3.7		
		Australia	*15.9*
Burma	37.7	*New Zealand*	*3.3*
North Korea	20.8		

Sources: International Economics Department, World Bank, *Recent Economic and Social Indicators* (Washington, D.C.: September 1987), pp. 4-6 (except Taiwan); *The Economist*, 27 February 1988, p. 30 (Taiwan).

Advances in domestic political stability were paralleled by significantly reduced tensions among many regional countries. The formation in 1967 of ASEAN (Association of Southeast Asian Nations) stimulated increasing cooperation, self-confidence, and solidarity among its members. The same period marked the beginning of the long, delicate process of reconciliation between Japan and the Republic of Korea—as diplomatic relations were established and a large-scale Japanese aid and investment program was initiated. It was in the '60s also that the break between the USSR and the PRC reached its decisive point, heightening tensions between the two Communist powers but, in its effects on their policies toward their neighbors, contributing in the longer run to the stability of the region. The Vietnam War, which intensified greatly in the '60s, did not disrupt the wider region's progress; and the end of American military involvement in Indochina in 1975, although traumatic, did not lead to the widely feared withdrawal of America from the region. Meanwhile, tensions between Hanoi and its communist neighbors increased.

The achievements of the past two decades have given rise to new challenges today. Having successfully pursued trade-oriented strategies of economic growth, the East Asian developing countries now see continuing success threatened by global trends—commodity price declines, protectionism, and heightened competition for markets. Trade frictions have moved to center stage in domestic politics on both sides of the Pacific and could come to shadow political relationships. Great differences in stages of economic development remain obstacles to the development of regional mechanisms for dealing collectively with economic problems. The global system—devised in the period of Atlantic dominance—has yet to adjust to the new economic prowess of East Asia, while some of the most successful East Asian economies are finding it difficult to adjust to the global responsibilities stemming from their economic achievements.

At the same time, the political institutions of the developing states of the region are facing new challenges. Long-time authoritarian leaders are approaching the end of their tenure in countries that lack regularized and tested succession procedures. Everywhere, members of a new, better-educated generation with changing values and aspirations are coming to the fore. And throughout the region, enhanced pressures for increased participation and diffusion of power are challenging patterns of authoritarianism and government control adopted in the past. The argument that new and developing countries cannot afford democratic freedoms has become less compelling as internal and external threats have become less potent and levels of education have risen. The argument that only au-

TABLE 2
GNP and GNP per capita of East Asian Countries
1986, with Trilateral and Oceania comparisons

	GNP[a]	GNP per capita[b]		GNP[a]	GNP per capita[b]
Japan	1,557.7	12,840	*Japan*	*1,557.7*	*12,840*
			EC	*2,800.0*	*8,688*
China	299.5	280	*USA*	*4,208.4*	*17,450*
			Canada	*351.8*	*13,730*
Northeast Asian NICs					
South Korea	98.4	2,370	*FRG*	*732.1*	*12,020*
Taiwan	95.1[c]	4,900[d]	*France*	*580.2*	*10,470*
Hong Kong	37.4	6,800	*UK*	*502.8*	*8,890*
			Italy	*413.9*	*7,240*
ASEAN			*Spain*	*186.7*	*4,.810*
Indonesia	83.9	510	*Netherlands*	*144.4*	*9,930*
Philippines	31.9	570	*Belgium*	*91.8*	*9,310*
Thailand	42.4	810	*Norway*	*63.6*	*15,280*
Malaysia	29.6	1,860	*Denmark*	*63.5*	*12,420*
Singapore	18.7	7,240	*Portugal*	*22.9*	*2,230*
Brunei	3.9[e]	17,570[e]	*Ireland*	*18.9*	*5,280*
			Luxembourg	*5.8*	*15,770*
Indochina					
Vietnam	n.a.	n.a.			
Kampuchea	n.a.	n.a.			
Laos	n.a.	n.a.			
			Australia	*170.1*	*10,670*
Burma	7.7	200	*New Zealand*	*23.1*	*7,060*
North Korea	n.a.	n.a.			

Sources: World Bank, *Recent Economic and Social Indicators,* pp. 4-6 (except Taiwan); *The Economist,* 27 February 1988, p. 30 (Taiwan).

[a]US$ billions   [b]US$ [c]GDP   [d]GDP per capita   [e]1985

thoritarian governments can maintain the order, discipline, and dedication to national purpose that economic development requires has become less persuasive as long and unchallenged tenure in some countries has magnified opportunities for corruption and entrenched bureaucratic power, and has discouraged flexible adaptation to changing requirements. The counterproductive impact of tight government controls has been underlined by the economic failures of Burma and the Communist states relative to the market economies, where considerable room for free enterprise has existed side by side with government planning and direction.

Significantly, pressures for more open political systems are coming primarily from the new, larger, and more sophisticated professional, technocratic, and business elites (increasingly possessing advanced degrees from leading Trilateral academic institutions) who have been both the product and the major beneficiaries of economic development. They continue to value stability and their desire is for evolutionary, not revolutionary, change. Indeed, in only two countries of the region does desire for change currently manifest itself in significant revolutionary movements. One is Burma, where economic advance has been stifled by the policies of an ideologically rigid and isolationist regime, and where national integration has been blocked by the uncompromising approach of the central government to demands of ethnic minority areas for greater autonomy. The other is the Philippines, where restored democratic government cannot quickly remedy the ills entrenched by Ferdinand Marcos' corrupt authoritarianism and disastrous economic policies.

Although the desire for political change is generally evolutionary, political transitions—even peaceful ones—are rarely accomplished without some turbulence. In more open systems, moreover, the appearance of turbulence is often heightened by the more pronounced criticism and overt agitation that freedom of expression permits, by the greater contentiousness of political parties when the prize for which they contest is real power, and by differences in motivation and perceived roles between parliaments and executive leaders. Once pressures for greater political participation become widespread, however, stubborn resistance is an equally likely cause of turbulence. In the new era in East Asia, this was amply demonstrated in the last years of the Marcos regime. The people of South Korea, by contrast, are beginning to fulfill their own aspirations for political participation under much more favorable circumstances, thanks to last-minute recognition by the government in June of 1987 that blocked evolution might well open the path to chaos or revolution.

Responsibility for adjusting to new requirements and taking advantage of new opportunities rests primarily with the East Asian developing countries themselves. Nevertheless, if the Trilateral countries recognize the value of the political evolution that is underway, they can adjust their policies and behavior in ways which can help create a generally favorable climate for positive change.

Chapter I of this report focuses on political evolution in the developing countries of East Asia. In this largely analytical chapter, we examine the links among political evolution, economic growth and the reduction of external threats. Governments have tended to be more responsive to pressures for economic liberalization than to demands for more open and participatory political processes, but political evolution is undeniably underway. The interests and roles of Trilateral countries in this evolution are touched upon briefly, in anticipation of later discussion in Chapter IV.

Chapter II is more policy-oriented, given its focus on issues of economic adaptation. The policy issues for Trilateral countries are more immediate here: How should global economic arrangements be adapted to reflect the rising strength and rising obligations of East Asia? How should the adaptation challenges for Japan, North America, and the European Community be approached? What policy adjustments can be requested of East Asian developing countries?

The security environment in East Asia—the focus of Chapter III—has been more benign in this decade than at any time since the end of World War II. Armed, non-guerilla conflict across borders is essentially limited to Indochina; the potential for such conflict remains significant only between the two Koreas. The advent of Mikhail Gorbachev in the Soviet Union raises interesting questions. While Western military strength must be maintained, it will also be important to seek ways to encourage a constructive Soviet role in the region.

Chapter IV brings together our policy conclusions and recommendations for the Trilateral countries.

I. Political Evolution

Economic Growth and Political Evolution
Authoritarianism, frequently under the auspices of charismatic leaders, has been the order of the day in much of developing East Asia for much of the postwar, post-colonial era, whether in the form of totalitarian rule by Communist parties or in the less tightly controlled pluralist systems typically dominated by the military or a single party. The longevity of these systems has reflected not only their monopoly of power, but also—at least in the early stages in some countries—some degree of popular support, or at least acquiescence, resting on the continued potency of traditional respect for authority and hierarchy (often laced with fear); on the perceived requirements for the survival of weak, new states in a disturbed and dangerous postwar world; and, in most successful East Asian developing countries, on the legitimacy rulers have won by their ability to deliver some degree of peace and prosperity to the ruled.

Paradoxically, while socio-political changes resulting from economic growth have contributed to stability, they have also contributed significantly to the growth of opposition to authoritarian rule and controls. On the one hand, stability has been supported by a much more generalized vested interest in the continued orderly functioning of state and society as standards of living have risen and confidence in continuing opportunity has grown. Stability has also been supported by the diffusion of education, which has made more plentiful and available the skills essential to the management of modern political and economic institutions. On the other hand, advances in well-being and education (including education in Trilateral countries), urbanization, travel, and the proliferation of modern media have expanded horizons, giving rise to demands (particularly among now much larger elites) for more open political systems and more meaningful political participation.

The socio-political changes that economic development has brought to much of East Asia reflect not only unusually high growth rates but also the extent to which the benefits of development have been distributed. This has been especially the case in the most rapidly developing countries—i.e., the "newly industrialized countries" (NICs). Singapore leads developing East Asia in the extent to which its citizens have achieved middle-class levels of disposable income and home ownership. (In 1986, for example, of the 85 percent of the population living in government-built housing, four-fifths owned their apartments.) Taiwan and the Republic of Korea are examples of more equitable than average income distributions, from which rural as well as urban dwellers have benefitted. Even in these countries, however, poverty has not been eliminated, while in countries lower on the per capita GNP scale, disposable incomes are still very low by Trilateral standards and a significant proportion of the population lives at or below the poverty line. Especially in Indonesia and the Philippines, where per capita GNP is only a little over $500, extremes of poverty contrast sharply with extremes of wealth. In these very densely populated countries, unemployment and underemployment are major problems; there and elsewhere, urbanization has proceeded much more rapidly than burgeoning cities can provide adequate housing, transportation, sanitary services, and the like.

A significant supplement, however, exists in most East Asian developing countries in the attention governments have given to strengthening a social infrastructure that has contributed significantly to the health, welfare, and education of the general population. Demographic data demonstrate the extent to which expanded social services, access to medical care and to safe water, better diet, and the like have compensated somewhat for low incomes and improved the circumstances of life for large numbers of people throughout the region. Life expectancy has risen markedly. Between 1965 and 1985 (see Appendix Table A-4), the increase was around ten years in most East Asian developing countries (and about fifteen years in China). Infant mortality statistics for the same period are equally impressive. The percentage of deaths in the first year per 1,000 births has fallen by about one-third in Indonesia and the Philippines, by about one-half in Thailand and Malaysia, and by more than half in China, the two Koreas, Taiwan, Hong Kong and Singapore (see Appendix Table A-4).

Perhaps no region of the world has shown greater respect and desire for education in recent years. This is especially true in the Sinic cultures. Expenditures for education as a percentage of GNP have risen steadily and virtually all children of primary school age are now in school in most of developing East Asia (see Appendix Table A-5). Secondary and higher education are also more accessible than in the past (see Appendix Table A-5). In ASEAN, this has been reflected in the doubling of administrative, managerial, and professional workers between 1970 and 1980. In the Republic of Korea, 26 percent of those of college age were enrolled in institutions of higher learning in 1984 as opposed to only 6 percent in 1965. Access to modern media—print and electronic—has also grown. In

South Korea, for example, almost 87 percent of all households own television sets.

In most of developing East Asia, appreciation of gains already made and confidence in further opportunity have significantly reduced the appeal of revolutionary demands for reordering state and society. To be sure, with stability having rested heavily on the ability of governments to deliver economic benefits, declining growth and shrinking opportunity could increase the attraction of radical doctrines, whether rooted in Maoism or religious fundamentalism. Thus far, however, demands for political change in developing East Asia have been primarily evolutionary. Their growth has reflected a new sense of entitlement among members of the now much larger and more influential entrepreneurial, managerial, and professional sectors. In the Philippines, for example, these middle-class elements played a major role in the events that dethroned Ferdinand Marcos and brought Corazon Aquino to the presidency. Again, in South Korea, in the spring of 1987, members of this burgeoning modern business/professional class showed their impatience with the pace of political development, even though they were to a considerable extent the beneficiaries of the system they sought to change. Among such groups in other countries of the region, there is considerable frustration with the limits on the authority of such representative institutions as exist. (Many of their members, it appears, are finding some outlet through cause-oriented, social service and advocacy organizations.) With the extraordinary new opportunities created by modern telecommunications, there is restiveness in increasingly literate and sophisticated societies with controls over public expression in and outside the media. Social and political controls—limitations on free speech and assembly, for example—are now less likely to be accepted as inevitable attributes of life and more readily charged to the shortcomings of unchecked leadership out of touch with the opportunities of today's world.

Among the younger generation also, especially among college youth, education and the wider dissemination of information have made for heightened awareness of political alternatives and increased restiveness with the restrictions of the status quo. The potency of student political activism, most recently demonstrated in South Korea, is not new in East Asia. A host of earlier examples of student participation come to mind beginning, in fact, with the nationalist movements of the colonial era and including such events as the overthrow of Syngman Rhee in 1960, of Soekarno in 1965, and of the Thanom-Praphat military dictatorship in 1973. Adding to the potential impact of student restiveness today, however, is not only the higher percentage of the relevant age group in higher education, as noted above, but also the youth bulge that characterizes the population structure. For example, almost 40 percent of the population of Southeast Asia and the Korean peninsula is under fifteen years of age.

Reduction of External Threats
Reduced preoccupation with strong external or externally supported threats to national independence and well-being, and consequent increases in self-confidence, have also contributed to pressures for broader political participation and greater government accountability. The projection of external Cold War rivalries into the region has become less intense and destabilizing. Increasing interest in Moscow and Beijing in good relations with non-Communist East Asian states has been reassuring, even though not necessarily seen as a permanent change of stance. Concerns over the consistency of American policy remain. However, immediate post-Vietnam War fears of U.S. withdrawal from East Asia have been largely dissipated, to the benefit of East Asian confidence and the detriment of Moscow's efforts to gain political influence from its considerably expanded military and naval presence in the region. Meanwhile, the evolution of closer and more cooperative relations among the non-Communist countries of the region has diminished preoccupation with threats from neighbors.

With the passage of time and changing circumstances, the threat posed to national governments and societies by domestic insurgencies (often externally supported) has receded significantly. Beijing and Moscow have largely abandoned their support for local Communist insurgents and subversive groups. Without external support and weakened by their own internal divisions, as well as by effective government countermeasures, Communist parties are no longer a significant factor in most of non-Communist East Asia. Only in Burma and the Philippines do Communist activities still constitute a significant threat to national governments and societies.

In the multi-ethnic nations of ASEAN, communal differences constitute a more obdurate problem, in some cases one that overlaps national boundaries. In the Philippines, the Muslims of the south continue to pursue autonomy or independence by means of military as well as political pressure, while similar, although much weaker, Muslim movements are active in Thailand's southern provinces; in Indonesia, political and economic frustrations are all too often expressed in localized violence against ethnic Chinese; in Malaysia, the delicate balance between the politically dominant Malay majority and the large and economically dominant Chinese minority is a constant preoccupation, its dangers accentuated by the rise among Malays of militant Muslim movements.

Even so, persistent deep-seated and sometimes conflicting ethnic allegiances within the ASEAN states have not precipitated racial disorder and violence on levels remotely approaching those currently characteristic of many other areas of the world. Similarly, the commitment of its members to ASEAN unity and strength has curbed tendencies, so evident elsewhere, to permit divergent ethnic identities to destroy cooperative bilateral relationships.

In the successful developing countries of Northeast Asia, as in ASEAN, economic growth and increased self-confidence have helped to moderate concern with external threats. South Koreans may remain preoccupied with the threat from the North but they no longer see themselves as significantly weaker. In Taiwan, confidence in continued viability has been bolstered by the achievements of the economy and the extensive external ties these achievements have fostered despite diplomatic isolation.

A more benign external climate and a less threatened domestic order have combined to make less compelling the arguments justifying authoritarianism as indispensable to national defense. Indeed, arguments that suppression of political opposition may in fact contribute to (rather than reduce) national weakness and vulnerability have gained weight from the events of recent years, especially in South Korea and the Philippines. In South Korea, continued suppression produced dramatically increasing echoes of North Korean propaganda in the student movement. In contrast, once the collective bargaining path was genuinely opened, the trade unions successfully resisted student efforts to radicalize their movement. In the Philippines, the Communist Party grew from an insignificant force in the late '60s to a major threat under Marcos. The weight of opinion in the executive and legislative branches of the U.S. government by 1985 was that the Communists' best chance of taking over the Philippines lay in the continuation in power of the Marcos regime.

The Adaptation Challenge
Heightened pressures for political change assume particular importance at a time when aging leadership (and the aging also of long-established institutions and accommodations) may in any case require alterations of existing arrangements. Considerable political power still lies in the hands of men who rose to prominence forty or more years ago in East Asia's nationalist revolutions and whose views were molded by developments of diminishing relevance to younger generations. Among this revolutionary generation, Ne Win, aged 76 and one of the Thirty Heroes who led Burma to independence, has ruled his country for over a quarter

of a century;[1] Soeharto, like Soekarno before him, is a member of the Generation of 1945, and at 66 has been Indonesia's leader for more than two decades; Lee Kuan Yew at 63 has been Prime Minister of Singapore since 1959; and Kim Il Sung at 75 has been North Korea's Great Leader for 40 years. Some members of this generation of leaders are showing themselves more responsive than their contemporaries to the forces of change, among them China's Deng Xiaoping and Vietnam's Nguyen Van Linh. But with the former aged 83 and the latter 71, the problem of succession arises as sharply in their countries as elsewhere in the region. Other long-time authoritarian rulers have already passed from the scene: Chiang Ching-kuo (1988), Ferdinand Marcos (1986), Park Chung Hee (1979), and Mao Zedong (1976).

The problem of institutional durability is also being raised more sharply in a number of countries. In Malaysia, where orderly constitutionally based transfers of power have been the post-independence rule, the various political party and communal arrangements that have supported continuity and stability have come under intense new pressure and may be fraying at the edges. The politically dominant Malays, whose unity in the United Malay National Organization (UMNO) has been the indispensable ingredient of orderly parliamentary government, remain in the throes of an unprecedented leadership struggle—a struggle accentuated by the confrontational style Prime Minister Mahathir has substituted for the consensual approach of his predecessors. UMNO's Chinese partner, the Malaysian Chinese Association (MCA), is in greater disarray than usual; and the Chinese opposition party (Democratic Action Party) is gaining at its expense. Meanwhile, the unwritten accommodation between Malays and Chinese that has been fundamental to communal peace is under challenge from the rise of militant Islam, changing Chinese attitudes, and the effects of a shrinking economic pie. A political crisis seriously disturbing Malaysia's ethnic peace is bound to have repercussions among its ethnically diverse neighbors.

In the small, highly respected city-state of Singapore, impatience with the pressure-cooker political atmosphere is growing, especially among the better educated and young. Lee Kuan Yew's political instrument, the Peoples' Action Party (PAP), can no longer count on the once automatic support of at least 75 percent of the voting population. In the 1984 elections, its share fell to 62.9 percent, a decline widely attributed to first-time voters (aged 21-24) who constituted 14 percent of the electorate in 1984, as opposed to 9 percent in 1968. Lee's detailed guidance, so brillliant for decades, is now open to increasing question from within and without.

---

[1] It is not at all clear that the end of the Age of Ne Win, with his resignation in July, will lead to any real changes in the near term.

In Thailand, still a different transition problem looms in the possibility of the voluntary abdication of King Bhumibol Adulyadej at a time of some uncertainty over the survival of civilian government. The king's talents and dedication, reinforcing the strong tradition of devotion to the monarchy, have made an important contribution to unity and stability in Thailand. The crucial question is whether the Crown Prince is capable of a similar role.

The East Asian Response

With the exception of South Korea, East Asian governments thus far have tended to be more responsive to pressures for economic liberalization than they have to demands for a more open and participatory politics. In the market economies, the growth in size and competence of the private sector and its links with the international economy have reduced both the requirement for and the acceptability of the high levels of government intervention that have existed side by side with the operation of market forces. Privatization programs have transferred publicly owned enterprises to private hands through sale of shares, transfer of management responsibilities, and outright divestiture. Central regulation is also being relaxed, particularly in the financial sector where banks and other financial institutions are being given greater leeway.

In the Communist states, where ideologically dictated policies have caused national economies to lag conspicuously behind those of the non-Communist developing countries, movement toward economic liberalization is taking on increasing momentum, although not without difficulties and continued long-standing problems. In Vietnam, Premier Nguyen Van Linh seems to be taking a leaf out of ASEAN's book in describing the regime's new economic approach. "Development of a country," he wrote in the November 1987 issue of an official Vietnamese journal, "depends to a very large extent on its capability to participate in international economic relations"—adding that, in "the new mechanism," both "planning and the use of the goods-money relationship" are important. In China, since 1977, economic liberalization can accurately be described as a revolution within a revolution. No country in the world has seen more dramatic changes in the last decade than China: the dissolution of the commune system and a return to family-centered agriculture; a good deal of autonomy for small and medium-sized industry; and practical recognition of the importance of profits and the availability of consumer goods in boosting productivity. Looking ahead, General Secretary Zhao Ziyang has predicted that, within two to three years, only about 30 percent of the economy will be controlled through central planning. And even in that most regimented of states, North Korea, revived interest in attracting foreign investment has opened up a still uncertain prospect of some loosening of state controls over the economy.

Liberalization in the political sphere has been a more halting process. In Communist countries, although Marxist-inspired economics may be increasingly abandoned, Leninist principles of party domination and discipline will not wither away. An increase in freedom of expression, whether under the banner of *glasnost* or *kaifang* or something else, must always have its limits in a Communist system. At their very core, Communist and Western systems still proceed from fundamentally different human values and notions of freedom.

In non-Communist countries also, overriding concerns with stability and with restraining potential sources of disorder persist among a leadership generation strongly influenced by memories of both the threats and instabilities of the first post-independence decades and the deficiencies of early experiments with Western-style democracy. Typifying these concerns, Lee Kuan Yew at the recent ASEAN Summit in Manila recalled the common experiences of his generation of ASEAN leaders. "They have experienced the disasters of World War II and the sufferings of three and one-half years of Japanese occupation. They have also experienced political strife and instability during the struggle for independence...[T]heir great experience was to struggle to preserve independence, to maintain national unity against Communist armed insurrections and against the divisive poles of different races, languages, and religions." Have the present leaders, he asks, succeeded in transmitting to the next generation "their values, habits, and attitudes of cooperation upon which stability, economic development and growth have taken place"? His answer to his own question suggests some skepticism. "Our young have no memories of past conflicts. They take the last 20 years of peace and prosperity as the normal course of events."

Ironically, Lee's concern about the fragility of the accomplishments of recent decades has led him to take conspicuously harsh measures against free expression which could erode his genuine accomplishments. These measures have been widely criticized, but the concerns that they reflect are shared by many members of developing East Asia's governing elites regardless of generation. They point to the threats still facing them: in South Korea of a military onslaught from the North; in Taiwan of a more aggressive PRC approach to reunification; in Malaysia of a bloody breakdown in communal relations; in Singapore of the perils of its existence as a tiny Chinese island in a Malay sea; and, in all the developing countries, the threat to social and political stability should their economies deteriorate seriously in an unfavorable international environment. These elites identify their countries with the democratic world.

Nevertheless, they still worry about how genuinely competitive political party systems—what they describe as 50%-plus-one decision-making—and untrammeled freedom of expression would interact with their own national traditions. Accepting in principle the desirability of political evolution, they see it as taking a course that will combine their own requirements and traditions with broader political participation in some new uniquely Asian mode.

That political evolution is already underway is undeniable; that it is moving toward some uniquely Asian model offering a more stable, orderly and representative future remains to be demonstrated; that it will be uninterrupted by reverses of one kind or another is unlikely. The apparent general public approbation for Marcos' 1972 declaration of martial law, as well as the accomplishments of his early years in absolute authority, seemed to some to verify arguments about the unsuitability of democracy to East Asia—but that was 16 years ago. For the Filipinos themselves, the return to democracy became an increasingly widespread objective, as was demonstrated in the strength and fervor of the popular movements opposing Marcos for some years before February 1986, as well as in the final events that swept him from power and replaced him with Corazon Aquino. The institutional foundations of restored democracy are now in place—a constitution and elected national and local governments—and freedom of expression is as untrammeled as it ever was in the past. At the same time, however, dissatisfaction with the pace of reform and recovery, restiveness in the military, and political violence are much in evidence, while Communist armed insurgency continues to pose a looming threat against which effective measures have yet to be devised.

In South Korea the change in the political environment has been of equal magnitude. In pursuing its new democratic experiment, the ROK enjoys advantages the Philippines lacks—an economy that continues to function effectively, the absence of armed insurgency within its borders, and the discipline imposed by consciousness of the threat looming across the DMZ. The outlook nevertheless remains uncertain. Much could happen that might prompt military efforts to restore autocratic government as a new president and a new assembly begin their terms, and institutions for local self-government are developed. Yet, what is truly remarkable is the widespread support that democracy seems to have in a country with no democratic traditions.

The situation in Thailand gives some credence to the notion that, in some nations, political evolution will result in new systems which, while more open and representative, will also be uniquely Asian. That this should be the case perhaps reflects Thailand's record—shared only with

Japan in Asia—of having escaped colonial or semi-colonial status and preserved its monarchical tradition intact. Certainly, its governing arrangements are difficult to describe in classic political science terms. Thailand is now credited with having a civilian government; but its leader, Prime Minister Prem Tinsulanond, became a civilian by retiring from the army (in which he had been commander-in-chief) before taking on political office. He has neither submitted himself to the electoral process nor taken the leadership of a political party; but he has served as the head of a constitutionally based government longer (since February 1980) than any of his predecessors since the establishment of Thailand's constitutional monarchy in 1932; his cabinet represents a coalition of political parties whose seats in parliament were won in free elections in 1986 (in which 60 percent of the eligible voters cast their ballots); and a free press engages enthusiastically in political debate. The army, meanwhile, continues to play an important role in politics as supporter of the government, executor of publicly funded social programs, critic of the venality and factionalism of political parties, and advocate of a decisive political role for appointed officials. Thus far during Prem's tenure, however, two coup attempts by army factions have been quickly put down and the army leadership has acquiesced in defeats for proposals intended to confine the authority of elected representatives.

Elsewhere in developing East Asia, the picture is more mixed. On the one hand, in Taiwan the martial law imposed in 1949 has been lifted, the opposition legitimized, and some greater freedom of expression permitted, including an evolving attitude towards contacts with the mainland. On the other hand, Malaysia and Singapore—which have preserved the forms of parliamentary government more consistently than other developing East Asian countries—have imposed restrictions on freedom of expression or political organization (or both) as rigorous as those that have long been characteristic of Soeharto's Indonesia.

Advances in one country and setbacks in another discourage generalization about the prospects for political openness in developing East Asia, especially when ASEAN's giant, Indonesia, has yet to be heard from. Two observations, however, apply fairly generally. First, in most countries, an institutional basis already exists for broadening political participation: increasingly literate citizenries have had the opportunity to vote in some form of general elections, however controlled they may be; legislative institutions are in existence, however limited their role; and, while the government party may hold the reins of power in its own hands, other parties exist and could become of greater importance in more open and competitive systems. Second, rising pressures for fuller political participation and greater freedom of expression are common to the region. Throughout the region also, such pressures originate most strongly from a significantly enlarged and better-educated middle class, including a growing cohort of university students. Except among some of the latter, and in wider circles in the Philippines, the demand is not for radical change; their objectives are evolutionary not revolutionary.

The Stake of the Trilateral Countries

Trilateral countries have much to gain from the satisfaction of these aspirations for peaceful evolution toward more participatory and accountable political systems. The remarkable strength and longevity of the North Atlantic Alliance and U.S.-Japan security ties have rested not only on common threat perceptions, but also, and to a far greater degree, on common attachment to political values which, however varied their institutional manifestations, are founded on respect for human rights and the expression of the general will through the open processes of representative government. The same values, if they are increasingly embodied in other East Asian political systems, will expand and strengthen their existing ties with Trilateral countries and provide a firmer basis in popular approval for the resolution of differences and for cooperation and mutual support.

No more in East Asia than in democracies elsewhere will evolution toward genuinely representative government provide guarantees against political divisiveness, leadership weakness, and conflicts among constituency interests that complicate domestic decision-making and the conduct of foreign relations. Indeed, the evolutionary process is rarely smooth. Under entrenched authoritarianism, on the other hand, seeming order can be bought at heavy cost. No less than in open societies, interest groups seek to shape state policy. But only those few with wealth, influence, or armed force at their disposal are likely to be successful and, where governments are not accountable and critical voices are silenced, corruption and intimidation may come to play the decisive role in the making and enforcement of government decisions. As the desire for fuller political participation increases, failure to respond can drive pressures for evolutionary change into revolutionary channels; the formidable growth of the Philippine Communist Party under the regime of Ferdinand Marcos is a striking example of this danger. Recent events in the ROK, on the other hand, illustrate how responsiveness and flexibility can overcome seeming dichotomies between freedom and order.

Although each country in the region must and will determine the shape of its own political institutions, the Trilateral countries can and should seek ways to encourage evolutionary trends. Patience and understanding will be required as growing pains seem to slow or disrupt the decision-making process. Continuing economic progress will facilitate peaceful political transitions. (Trilateral roles and responsibilities in this regard are outlined later.) Trade frictions must not be allowed to work against long-range political and strategic interests. Educational and informational exchange, the provision of training opportunities, cooperation among non-governmental organizations, contacts among parliamentarians, humanitarian and technical assistance in areas where it is still required, all make important contributions to both economic and political development. Attempts to exercise influence on a government-to-government basis raise more difficult problems. Pursued too vigorously, such attempts can arouse hostile nationalist reactions, even among those whose interests they seek to serve. Pursued with sensitivity and tact, however, they can make positive contributions to the evolutionary process.

II. Economic Adaptation

The Rise of East Asia

The emergence of East Asia as a major center of international manufacturing, commerce, and finance seems likely to be recorded by future economic historians as one of the most remarkable developments of the last third of the twentieth century. Industrial production in this region has been growing by leaps and bounds; manufacturing prowess has spread from its original Asian center in Japan to the NICs, the ASEAN countries, and China.

Japan has become the second largest economy in the world. At current exchange rates (though not in purchasing power terms), GNP per capita in Japan exceeds that in the United States. The current aggregate value of stocks quoted on the Tokyo Stock Exchange exceeds that of the New York Stock Exchange.

The four NICs—Singapore, Hong Kong, Taiwan, and South Korea— each have attained a marked level of affluence. The GNP per capita of each of the four has grown beyond the first tier of OECD members (Portugal and Turkey). Singapore and Hong Kong have surpassed (and Taiwan has reached) the next tier of OECD member countries (Spain, Ireland, Greece). Hong Kong has surpassed Rotterdam as the world's busiest container port.[1] South Korea is catching up with Japan as the world's foremost shipbuilder.

ASEAN increasingly advances common negotiating positions vis-à-vis Japan and in multilateral negotiations. Mutually beneficial opportunities, growing personal trust, and institutionalized dialogue and cooperation are making ASEAN the second most successful community of nations after the European Community. However, trade relations with two outsiders, the United States and Japan, are still far more significant than trade among ASEAN member countries themsleves; and gaps in income levels and in the stages of industrial development are much larger than within the EC. The combined population of the ASEAN countries (about 280 million, of which nearly 60 percent is concentrated

---

[1] "Vintage port," *The Economist*, 20 February 1988, p. 74.

in Indonesia) is not far behind the EC (about 320 million), but the ASEAN GNP is less than one-tenth of the EC's and only about two-thirds of Canada alone.

The combined GNP of the Northeast Asian NICs, the ASEAN countries, and China is still less than half that of Japan alone. Yet China's long-range effect on the international economic system, by early in the next century, could be profound. If per capita Chinese exports, presently slightly above $30, were to achieve only one-tenth (approximately $200 per person) of the current Japanese level,[2] the rest of the world would have to contend with a challenge similar to the magnitude of the current challenge posed by Japan's advance (since China is ten times more populous than Japan). Given its size and sense of its own importance, an industrializing China will call for formidable adjustment efforts by all parties concerned. The mode of mutual adaptation between the rest of East Asia and the Trilateral countries in the 1990s could become a precedent for the later adaptation between China and the rest of the world, despite continuing differences between China's political institutions and those of other East Asian countries.

Changing Trilateral Involvement

The continued economic and political development of East Asia is in the interest of the Trilateral countries, in the most fundamental sense. The growth of the economies of the region increases living standards in the region and in its trading partners. The Trilateral nations benefit from greater consumer choices and competitive pressures to increase efficiency in their own industries. At the same time, the continued economic advance of the region obviously presents major issues of economic adaptation to the Trilateral countries—trade friction is inevitable—and to the international economic arrangements of which the Trilateral countries have been the principal custodians.

The postwar era saw a retreat of European political influence from the East Asia/Pacific region, with the British, French, Dutch, and Portuguese (as well as the Americans) all relinquishing long-treasured colonial possessions. In recent years, led by trade and business opportunities, European interest has begun to revive—but still remains hampered by parochialism and unwillingness to take risks in challenging markets, as well as by an overall lack of political will and vision to exploit the

---

[2]This is a hypothetical level, not a considered projection for a particular time. Much lower export levels will still present a significant challenge. The value of China's exports grew at an annual rate of 9.5 percent in 1980-86. Assuming a constant population in China, it would take 21 years of 9.5 percent growth for the $30 per capita level to reach $200, without allowance for inflation. With adjustment for inflation, the time period would be considerably longer.

opportunities offered by this dynamic region. This is especially ironic given the fact that European involvement in the region is now welcomed by the smaller economies as a potentially important counterweight to excessive dependence on or domination by the United States and Japan. *The challenge for Western Europe is simple: to reestablish an active presence in the world's most dynamic region.*

Canada's trade across the Pacific now exceeds its trade with Europe. Canada receives more immigrants from Asia than from any other region (more than 40 percent of the total in 1985), and the majority of foreign students currently enrolled in Canada come from Asia-Pacific countries.[3] The government is actively seeking to expand Canada's presence in the region. Economic relations have been the primary but not exclusive focus.

Japan has emerged as the most important source of capital, concessional assistance, technology, and imports for other countries in the region. Though an economic giant in the region (and the world), Japan has been politically modest. Tokyo rarely attempts to present a philosophy of managing the global or regional economies in a comprehensible format or in a consistent and viable package involving clear target-setting and specific policy supports. Japan will need to become the principal absorber of the manufactured exports of the rest of the region over the next decade—an American role heretofore—and this will entail some difficult political decisions. Above all, *Japan will need to accept more of the responsibilities that come with such a preeminent role.* Several suggestions are contained in this report; others will emerge once the basic concept is accepted.

The influence of the United States spread over the region in the postwar era. In fulfilling its view of its global responsibilities, the United States fought its two major wars of the last 40 years in East Asia. The rise of U.S. interest in East Asia and the Pacific is both a result and a cause of the economic dynamism in most of the region—a dynamism which, within the United States, has contributed to the shift of the economic center of gravity toward the West.[4] For the United States, as for Canada, two-way trade across the Pacific has surpassed trade with Europe. For both countries, the Far East has become the "Near West."

Through most of the postwar era, in East Asia as elsewhere, the United States has been the principal buttress of a multilateral approach to the

---

[3] Paul M. Evans, "A New Pacific Strategy for Canada? Problems and Prospects," in Bernard T. K. Joei, ed., *Canada and the Pacific* (Taipei: Centre for Area Studies, Tamkang University, forthcoming).

[4] The ports of Los Angeles and Long Beach handled 58.6 million tons of cargo in 1986, surpassing the 21 million that moved through the Port of New York and New Jersey. "Special Report: The Pacific Century," *Newsweek*, 22 February 1988, p. 57.

international trading system and international economic management more generally. Current U.S. bilateralism raises concerns about the path of American adjustment to international economic change and presents an urgent question for the region: Should Japan and other East Asian nations follow the Canadian model in dealing with the United States and seek, as many see it, a privileged position inside a giant economic zone? We believe the 1988 U.S.-Canada bilateral free trade agreement can be a giant step towards a broader, global free trade system. On the other hand, there are fairly widespread fears in East Asia that bilateralism may undermine multilateral progress and democratic management of the international trade regime. We think these fears are exaggerated, but they will persist until proven wrong by events over the next several years.

Economics and Politics

Two other points should be made in this introductory section. The first recalls the previous chapter—namely, the connection between economic growth and economic liberalization on one hand, and political liberalization on the other. Economic growth is often a critical (although not sufficient) condition for the relaxation of government controls and the development of stable participatory political systems—particularly in East Asia, where traditional attitudes and value systems usually give more emphasis than Western cultures do to respect for authority and to obligations to family and other primary groups, and less emphasis to individual rights. Freer and more open economic systems not only encourage economic growth, but also require (hence lead to) a freer flow of information among individuals. At the same time, they promote decentralized decision-making, an essential condition of modern democracy. Even in socialist states, domestic deregulation and external liberalization are linked, and form an essential prerequisite for a more open society. Pluralism suffocates where allocation of economic resources remains in the hands of a few. An externally closed economic system spawns oligarchy, especially in fledgling democracies.

Second, continued economic development is raising serious issues of adaptation for the East Asian developing countries themselves. While East Asia's strength lies in the strong competitiveness of its exports, its excessive dependence on exports beyond the region is also a weakness, especially exports to the United States with its chronic trade deficit. East Asia has to depend more on intra-East Asian trade and on the consumption of middle-income citizens in the region. The process will be only gradual, and the adaptations must be mutual.

The Adaptation Challenge for Global Economic Arrangements
While bilateral approaches cannot be totally rejected, the multilateral economic institutions established since World War II (especially the IMF, IBRD, GATT, and OECD) remain the underpinnings of the global economic system. Regional and bilateral arrangements should only be transitional or temporary aids for strengthening the global regime.

Over time, the existing powers in the global regime will need to acknowledge the rise of East Asia by increasing the role and status (voting rights, high offices, etc.) of the region in international institutions in a manner commensurate with the economic power of East Asian countries and in proportion to their willingness to accept the obligations which come with a greater role. The political, legal, and business cultures in much of East Asia are different from those presupposed by the existing international institutions at the time of their formation, but this additional aspect of mutual adaptation is facilitated as the values of democracy and more or less market-oriented economies are now more widely accepted than at any time in recent years.

Most East Asian economies crucially depend on trade for growth, and can upgrade their domestic standards of living only under a global system which remains relatively open. The need to avoid bilateralism and economic "bloc-ism" will put strong pressure on these countries to open their own markets, adjust their exchange rates more smoothly, and support multilateral and global institutions more firmly. East Asian nations, as trading nations and borrowers of concessional development finance, have been beneficiaries of these institutions. As their economies have grown in importance, their stake in a stable international economic order has increased proportionately. With this rise in their stake, they can now be expected to begin to make positive contributions, instead of merely remaining recipients of benefits. Hence, their positive participation should be encouraged by the Trilateral nations. Peer review, dispute settlement, and policy coordination within various global and regional institutions should be strengthened.

The OECD
The current composition of the Organization for Economic Cooperation and Development is out of date for a global grouping of economically advanced democratic countries with major stakes and major roles in the international economy. Aside from European Community members, Japan, the United States and Canada, the current OECD membership is limited to seven other European countries, Australia and New Zealand.

Some argue, implicitly at least, that the OECD should be a regional not global organization. They look toward a separate "Pacific OECD" in the years to come. We welcome the efforts made toward greater economic cooperation in the Pacific region (see Appendix B), but our primary concern is the successful functioning of the global economy, in which we believe the OECD has a role to play, particularly in the process of "peer review" that over time will help lay the groundwork for more substantial cooperation. To fulfill this role in the current international economy calls for some expansion of OECD membership in East Asia.

The four NICs are the main candidates. Their levels of industrialization, per capita GNP, and modes of participation in the international economy (relatively liberal external economic policies, and major participation in trade in manufactures) make them complex modern economies. They are among the top 25 exporting countries and top 25 exporters of manufactures (see Appendix Tables A-2 and A-3); and Taiwan, Hong Kong and South Korea are among the top 15.

Overarching political questions make it impossible for Taiwan or Hong Kong to become OECD members without the blessing of Beijing, though such blessing is not inconceivable. (Hong Kong is now a member of GATT and Taiwan's possible GATT membership is under discussion. Both participate in the Asian Development Bank, along with Beijing.) The size of Singapore's economy may make it too small for OECD membership, and there are concerns in many Trilateral countries about the current political climate in Singapore.[5]

South Korea should be invited to join the OECD. 1988 would be a propitious year to begin the process leading to South Korea's entry in the early 1990s, especially following the recent presidential and legislative elections.[6] South Korea is fast becoming one of the world's most efficient producers of steel, automobiles, and electronic products, and is matching Japan, as noted above, as the leading shipbuilding nation. It should become a substantial ODA donor nation in the 1990s, and also the first non-resource-rich country with a chronic trade surplus vis-à-vis Japan.

Japan is unable to offer advice to South Korea for historical reasons, and, despite its continuing influence, U.S. relations with South Korea have also become tense at those times when America's bilateral pressures on the trade and investment fronts have been perceived as unfair or too tough. It seems likely that we are now headed into such a phase, given domestic pressures in the United States and the consequences of a more

---

[5] Some argue that it is hypocrisy to make democracy one of the tests of OECD membership now (recalling earlier non-democratic regimes in Spain, Portugal, Greece and Turkey while in the OECD). We recognize these earlier exceptions, but believe this criterion is now more firmly established.

[6] 1988, the year of the Seoul Olympiad, is also symbolically important. Japan joined the OECD in 1964, the same year Japan hosted the first Olympiad in Asia. South Korea's current GNP per capita is well above Japan's figure for 1964, after adjustment for inflation.

independent National Assembly in Korea. Such are the by-products of the more democratic society we all applaud, but in such circumstances, South Korea would benefit from and might be receptive to peer reviews in multilateral forums such as the OECD. Like its neighboring industrial democracy, the representatives of South Korea might bring back home a more internationally oriented sense of policy direction from international organizations, and gradually integrate their national economy into the international economy.[7]

The GATT and International Trading Arrangements
The multilateral trading arrangements developed under the auspices of the General Agreement on Tariffs and Trade have been jolted by Japan. No world trading system can absorb indefinitely such swift changes in comparative advantage. The GATT regime can be politically sustained only when the changes effectuated by new players are within the absorptive capacity of large established players. This capacity is determined by innate social flexibility and institutional means to cushion the impact. Absorptive capacity can be stretched somewhat by adjustments in macroeconomic and microeconomic policies, but not indefinitely.

Japan has adopted voluntary export restraints (VERs) vis-à-vis various trading partners. These first served as an emergency exit through the GATT wall created by the most-favored-nation (MFN) principle, but this emergency exit has become, through repeated use, a well-trodden path. These and other bilateral deals have undermined the GATT, but without them, the aggrieved trading partner might have taken much more protectionist measures (in steel, automobiles, and color TVs) for a longer period of time, damaging recent rounds of GATT negotiations at the same time. Such bilateral deals have been justified in Japan by a unique political situation (i.e., the unilateral security umbrella of the United States over Japan, Japan's sense of being a new member of the "club,"

---

[7] In recommending that South Korea be invited to join the OECD, we recognize the concern of some that the OECD is in danger of becoming too large and formal to serve its purpose as a flexible framework for discussion. Greater use of subgroups relevant to the issues at hand seems to be a way to assure the needed flexibility as the membership somewhat expands. South Korea and Brazil were involved in particular OECD subgroups in the late 1970s, and this method could also be used now to reach beyond the membership at times. Yugoslavia is now associated with some activities. (See Appendix C.) What about Brazil and a few other key developing countries outside East Asia as OECD members? South Korea has become a democratic industrialized market economy of substantial economic size, the type of country the OECD should include on a global basis. Brazil is larger, but its per capita GNP is considerably lower than the $3,000 threshold we would recommend. A size criterion, noted above in relation to Singapore, would exclude some others with relatively high per capita GNP. Some oil-exporting countries are of substantial economic size, with relatively high per capita GNP, but their economies are not modern industrial market economies of the OECD type, and some are not democracies. We realize that not all current OECD members meet all of these criteria, but they should not have their memberships revoked.

Japan's perception of market dependency). How East Asian NICs, ASEAN countries, and China would adjust trade relations if there were emergencies with the United States and other Trilateral countries—when the underlying political conditions might not be the same—is a question which faces the GATT.

The safeguard clause that GATT now provides (Article 19) can bring only temporary relief and is not crafted to address the structural adjustment called for by the rise of sustained "winners." Compensation is an unrealistic political proposition for a country with a chronic trade deficit, while selective safeguards will kill MFN, a cardinal principle of the GATT. Though not sanctioned under GATT rules, voluntary export restraints have conveniently taken the wind from the sails of protectionist trade bills. Nevertheless, VERs should not spread further, and should be used only sparingly. A remodelled and widely accepted safeguard rule and notification of voluntary export restraints (allowing for more transparency) are each a must. Safeguard measures when taken should be phased out over time. After a certain amount of time, monitoring or examination by a third party may be effective.

A bilateral or regional agreement is generally put forward as an interim stage in the process of reaching a multilateral goal, but may end up becoming an objective in itself. The experience of the EC's Common Agricultural Policy suggests that the policy of a limited group tends to be less liberal than that of individual, fairly liberal member countries. Industry-specific arrangements tend to survive their original economic raison d'etre by dint of the political clout of vested interests the arrangements help to create. The Multi-Fiber Agreement is an example and should be phased out. The Trilateral countries should take particular caution to mold and manage bilateral and regional arrangements to be compatible with the eventual global free trade regime.

Many of the subjects taken up in the current GATT round—including intellectual property rights, service trade, and TRIM (trade-related investment measures)—are so new that sufficient facts and figures must be collected and conceptual frameworks and negotiating principles are not yet defined. Somewhat preempting the negotiations, the United States has pressed some East Asian countries (Malaysia, South Korea, Singapore, and Thailand, among others) into changing their systems of legal protection for intellectual property and the services market (e.g., Korean insurance). While such exercises may make the "playing field" more "level" for the United States, they have, at times, also created new distortions under the GATT regime.

The NICs and ASEAN have shown much stronger interest in the Uruguay Round than in the past rounds of multilateral negotiations. The aggressiveness of the U.S. negotiating stance is a factor here, and U.S. bilateralism is another. The elimination of GSP (Generalized System of Preferences) privileges by the United States for the East Asian NICs as of January 1989, an unavoidable U.S. decision, has made the NICs aware that the United States will treat mature economies as such.

Many developing countries have regarded GATT as a "rich man's club" and have felt more affinity towards UNCTAD (United Nations Conference on Trade and Development). However, East Asian developing countries have recently recognized that GATT rules give countries rights to resist unilateral demands. Hong Kong, Singapore, and South Korea have formally accepted most of the six GATT codes elaborated in the Tokyo Round covering non-tariff measures—subsidies and countervailing duties, government procurement, and the like (see Appendix Table A-12). Other ASEAN countries are largely outside the codes, but Thailand has been quite active in the Cairns Group (formed to demand an end to heavy subsidies for EC and American agricultural products), which helped ensure the inclusion of agricultural trade issues in the Uruguay Round.[8] Taiwan is not now a member of the GATT—while largely receiving MFN treatment from its major trading partners—but the possibilities are being explored.

China will participate in the Uruguay Round, although only in limited areas. Intellectual property rights, trade in services, government procurement, agriculture, anti-dumping and countervailing duties are probably among the areas China has yet to take up. Eventually the Trilateral countries must seek common competition rules with countries such as China where domestic markets are organized differently from the type the GATT regime has presupposed. Finding a way to absorb Chinese exports will be important in the 1990s. The GATT may be heavily tested if China's industrialization succeeds, but the political stability of the region may be undermined if China fails.

East Asian countries with trade surpluses should work much harder to open their domestic markets, for services as well as for goods.[9] Progressive liberalization in financial, capital and foreign exchange markets is urgently needed as well.

---

[8] This is presently a group of 13 (one member, Fiji, recently bowed out from the original 14 countries) formed in August 1986 at Cairns, Australia, to promote freer, unsubsidized agricultural trade. Members include Australia, New Zealand, Canada, the ASEAN countries (minus the Philippines and Brunei), Argentina, Colombia, Brazil, Uruguay, Chile, and Hungary.

[9] A mercantilistic trade policy and a balance of payment surplus are generally unrelated. Macroeconomic management and exchange rates are much more critical determinants of the current account balance. The perception of unsullied trade policy conduct, however, is necessary to take leadership and initiative in multilateral negotiations.

International Financial Arrangements and the IMF and World Bank
Trilateral countries, the United States in particular, should be careful not
to put an inordinately large portion of the burden on exchange rate
changes for reducing current payments imbalances. The stock market
events of October 1987 showed clearly the close link between foreign
exchange markets and stock markets, as well as the degree of integration
among national financial markets. In East Asia and beyond, the danger
that exchange rate instability may lead to confusion in stock and bond
markets and eventually bring the world economy into a prolonged
recession is now universally acknowledged.

East Asia is particularly vulnerable to an unstable dollar since the
countries in East Asia are heavily dependent on the U.S. dollar as a trade
vehicle. Even Japan is using yen for only 30-40 percent of its exports and
about 10 percent of its imports.[10] Oil and many other commodities are
quoted in dollars, and East Asian dependence on the U.S. market for
export sales is generally high.

The question of a wider international role for the the yen is a pertinent
item on the economic agenda of the 1990s. For borrowers and lenders as
well as for traders, elimination of exchange rate risk and stability of
interest rates are of paramount importance. A more universal use of the
yen would advance these purposes and allow more latitude in selection
of yardsticks to accurately calculate return on investment, yield on
financial instruments, and margins for export and import transactions on
both sides of the trading table. For this purpose, Japan's financial markets
for short-term government bonds, commercial paper, and other instruments and products must be free of regulations, and interest rates have
to reflect market conditions in and outside Japan. Also, as the largest
creditor nation, Japan must fully integrate its markets internationally so
that the world economy functions more smoothly.

Japan and Germany are located at the eastern and western frontiers of
the free world. The fact that Japan is an island nation at the periphery of
a security zone—far away from the core country of Trilateral security, the
United States—and Japan's resource vulnerability, are among the psychological factors which, at least in the minds of the Japanese, limit the
yen's role. The dollar's role as a reserve asset of central banks has
declined from around 75 percent during the latter half of the 1970s to
about 50 percent of foreign exchange holdings by the end of 1986 (ECU
12.2%, D-mark 12.1%, yen 5.9%); but the yen (and the German mark) will
only supplement not replace the U.S. dollar as the key currency. As an

---

[10] West Germany uses German marks for up to 80 percent of its exports and 40-50 percent of its imports.

investment vehicle currency, the yen is becoming the second-ranking currency (though still a distant second) after the U.S. dollar, especially in bond issuance, external bank borrowing, and so forth. To play a bigger role, the yen must be supported by more internationally integrated capital and financial markets, and by a richer diversity of yen-denominated assets which offer higher profitability, safety, and liquidity.[11] The cost of raising funds must be low and assets must be completely negotiable. Non-inflationary macroeconomic management which ensures the domestic value of, and therefore confidence in, the yen is a natural assumption. Tokyo is acquiring these conditions, but not fully. It has to be internationalized in all senses, including linguistic ability and efficient support services (legal, accounting, consulting, secretarial, offices, etc.), reasonable communication and transportation costs, openness in official and private information access, and so on.

The NICs with chronic current account surpluses should allow their exchange rates to adjust more smoothly over time to the underlying strength of their economies. The experience of the highly regulated Tokyo foreign exchange market in 1971 should be instructive. This experience clearly shows that market forces will penetrate foreign exchange controls, and a drastic currency realignment (of the dam-burst type) may be triggered at some point.

East Asian countries have had limited influence in the policymaking process at the IMF and World Bank. The relatively weak position of Japan and East Asian countries generally is reflected in the small number of senior positions and/or the low voting rights which they hold in these organizations, as well as in most UN Specialized Agencies.[12] There are a number of reasons for this, including the belief by East Asians that their career possibilities are limited within the prevailing Anglo-Saxon organizational culture and a handicap in required language skills. North American and European domination of these institutions has been reflected in their leadership; the World Bank has always been headed by an American and the IMF by a European. (When the position of IMF Managing Director became vacant in 1986, a few Japanese were rumored to be under consideration.) Japan is the leading edge of East Asian involvement in the international financial institutions, but it still shies away from policy initiatives and has largely supported these institutions

---

[11] See the speech by Yoshio Terasawa at the *International Herald Tribune* Centennial Conference, November 11-13, 1987, in Singapore.

[12] Voting power in the IMF and World Bank is discussed further in Chapter IV. Japan's shares in the World Bank were increased in 1986 beyond any single West European country, along with a $450 million supplementary contribution by Japan to the World Bank's International Development Association.

through financial contributions. The Asian Development Bank (ADB) is the only institution where Japan has dominated in both financial contributions and senior positions, but in consideration of regional sensitivities, even the ADB is not headquartered in Japan. As East Asian economies play a larger role in international finance and aid-giving, they should be offered a proportionately greater role in both senior personnel and policymaking.

**Adaptation Challenges for
Trilateral Countries and Developing East Asia**

How do we build sustainable relationships of interdependence? The recent tensions between the United States and Japan show that a perception of excessive dependence by one country on another is unhealthy for international cooperation. Factors which produce such perceptions include: trade dependence on a single export market or import source, unilateral protection by the nuclear umbrella of one other country, reliance on a single other currency as the vehicle for trade and investment and as a reserve asset, reliance on foreign savings from one particular country or acquisition by interests from that country of a significant amount of landmark real estate.[13] A perception of excessive dependence can produce emotional reactions which in turn stimulate nationalism or isolationism and provide a psychological launching pad for protectionism. Such perceptions are easily fueled by a sense of unfairness, and trigger moral, or at least political, indignation.

Stable international relationships between nation-states at this present stage of development are only sustainable by a general perception of symmetry. Asymmetry is tolerated when the difference in economic strength justifies it. But when a party shows signs of becoming an equal in economic strength, one natural development would be the evolution of a cooperative agreement for sharing the costs of maintaining the status quo more commensurate with relative economic strength. If this is not perceived to be done sufficiently, one feels that other forms of compensation are in order. The value of such compensation, however, looks different to the payer and the payee, and both sides end up feeling they received the short end of the agreement. Troubles start here.

How to build sustainable relationships of interdependence remains the central challenge of adaptation in this as well as in other regions.

---

[13]One can easily argue that these notions are unreasonable. Just as the United States feels dependent on Japan's savings, Japanese lenders and investors feel dependence on their U.S. debtors. Japan feels dependent on the U.S. market just as the Americans are feeling dependence on Japan as the import source. But the unreasonable perception is an important real factor which needs to be addressed.

Japan

Japan faces a particularly acute challenge in its economic relations with the rest of East Asia. Japan's share of the NIC's exports has been far below that of the United States. Up until the recent dramatic rise in the value of the yen relative to the dollar, Japan's trade with the NICs had been dominated by a pattern of raw material and light manufactures imports and capital goods exports. Japan must now become the principal absorber of exports of manufactured products from the rest of the region. Since the appreciation of the yen vis-à-vis the dollar is so much greater than the appreciation of other East Asian currencies, Japanese manufacturing investments in and sourcing of manufactured and semi-manufactured goods, parts, and components from the NICs and Thailand have increased sharply to preserve the international competitiveness of Japanese corporations. Imports into Japan from these countries are rapidly increasing.[14]

Japan was dazzling in catching up with the West. Now it has to learn to let the East Asian NICs catch up with it. There naturally will be resistance to this in Japan. The NICs have sought to allay the suspicions of North America and Europe that they may prove to be as disturbing as Japan has been. Differences with Japan in size of economy, technology level, and R and D capability are enormous; but similarities—e.g., Confucian culture, emphasis on education, quality of labor—are also obvious. Japan's manufacturing investments and licensed production in the East Asian NICs will make the connection clearer.

Japan's policy directions—including its Uruguay Round strategy, and its modes of accommodation in the region as well as towards North America and Europe—will exert a broad influence on how the other Trilateral regions respond to East Asia as a whole.

Western Europe

Western Europe has insulated itself more than North America or Japan from the impact of the East Asian developing economies. And for this same reason, Europe has benefitted less. Japan and the developing countries of East Asia account for only about seven percent of European Community imports and four percent of its exports. On the other hand, Western Europe has been significantly involved in the East Asian region as an aid donor, providing considerably more ODA than the United States (see Appendix Table A-9).

---

[14] In U.S. dollar terms, Japanese imports from South Korea increased by 52.7 percent in 1987 over 1986. From Taiwan, imports increased by 51.9 percent; from Hong Kong, 45.4 percent; from Singapore, 40.7 percent; and from Thailand, 29.2 percent. As this occurs, the percentage of manufactures in total Japanese imports also increases—it passed 40 percent in 1987 and is near 50 percent now.

Discriminatory quotas against East Asian goods are found in European markets, partly as a legacy of the price Japan and other East Asian countries paid to Europe in order to be admitted into the GATT. More recently, various means (voluntary export restraints, tariff increases, etc.) have also been employed to protect European markets. They should be negotiated away in exchange for liberalizing steps taken by East Asian trading partners.

The principal challenge for Western Europe lies in reestablishing an active presence in the world's most dynamic region. As already noted, a greater European presence is strongly desired in much of the region to reduce economic dominance by Japan and the United States. Moreover, Europe cannot sit idly by and let its main competitors—the North American countries and Japan—monopolize the ample business and economic opportunities in the region. Historical, cultural, religious, and business ties abound between East Asia and Europe. *Europe should participate more vigorously on all fronts in the region.* This requires a long-term strategic view by European leaders of the importance of East Asia, precisely what is currently lacking.

The United States and Canada
As noted above, for both Canada and the United States, trade across the Pacific now exceeds trade with Europe. In 1986, 60 percent of Canada's two-way trade (excluding trade with the United States) was with Japan, developing Asia, and Oceania. Canada has traditionally had a surplus in its trade with Japan and developing East Asia, but that surplus rapidly declined in recent years and became a significant deficit in 1986 (see Appendix Table A-7 for bilateral trade balances with individual East Asian developing countries). A more abiding Canadian concern has been the composition of this trade, particularly the dominance of commodities in Canadian exports.[15] The government has devoted particular effort to expanding exports of manufactures and processed goods, within an overall effort to expand Canadian trade in East Asia. Since 1984 two government policy papers have emphasized Canada's priority interests in the Pacific area and a variety of public and private institutional links have been developed. Canada has been an active participant in the Pacific Economic Cooperation Conference.

The United States has been running tremendous deficits in its trade with East Asia, particularly with Japan and the three Northeast Asian

---

[15]The composition issue also relates to regional differences within Canada. The Western provinces have traditionally been the source of a large percentage of Canadian exports to East Asia, while manufacturing concerns in Ontario and Quebec have competed against East Asian imports. More balance in expanded Canadian economic relations with East Asia will usefully raise the stakes of Ontario and Quebec in these relations.

NICs. These deficits have fed strong protectionist pressures in the United States and strong criticism of East Asian trading partners. One important development in early 1988, noted above, was the U.S. announcement of removal of the four East Asian NICs from its Generalized System of Preferences as of the beginning of 1989. Part of the challenge for the United States is to distinguish more clearly between legitimate requests to make of its East Asian economic partners and ones that more properly belong to U.S. macroeconomic management. Ideally, the United States will negotiate away existing restrictions (MFA and various VERs) when and if its East Asian trading partners take liberalizing steps in their own markets, rather than threaten additional protectionist measures.

The signing of the Canada-U.S. free trade agreement has aroused great interest in East Asia. There are two main East Asian concerns. One is about possible negative effects on the progress of the multilateral liberal trading system, concerns which we believe are rather exaggerated, as noted above. Canada took the initiative for this agreement. Both sides point out that the arrangement is fully in line with Article XXIV of the GATT and is intended to be trade-creating rather than trade-diverting. They stress that the bilateral negotiations and agreement do not imply any less interest in the current round of multilateral trade negotiations, where both countries are prepared to negotiate improved access to their respective markets. Moreover, the agreement "holds the potential to set useful precedents for multilateral negotiations in such vital areas as trade in services and trade-related investment measures."[16]

The second concern of East Asian countries is whether they should also seek such bilateral arrangements with the United States. There has been some discussion of a U.S.-Japan version or a U.S.-ASEAN version. For Japan and other East Asian countries such bilateral arrangements with the United States would encourage increases in an already uncomfortable degree of dependence on the U.S. market. A Japan-U.S. agreement in particular would alienate other Asian countries and perhaps inevitably draw attention away from the Uruguay Round of multilateral trade negotiations, in which success is urgently needed. Because of the disparate nature of the ASEAN countries and their dissimilarity with the countries of North America, it is not clear that the arrangement negotiated between Canada and the United States would be a model for an ASEAN-U.S. agreement. The Japan-U.S. relationship does not match the Canada-U.S. relationship in terms of degree of involvement with the American economy.

---

[16] This passage is taken from the speech of Joe Clark, Canada's Secretary of State for External Affairs, to the 1987 Trilateral Commission annual meeting, as printed in *The San Francisco Meeting of the Trilateral Commission, March 1987* (New York: 1987).

The Developing Countries of East Asia
The smooth integration of the rapidly growing developing economies of
East Asia into the world economic system also requires major adjustments in these countries, especially the four East Asian NICs. These
economies have been engaged in a process of "catch-up" growth. For
most of them—China is the exception—exports have been the engine of
growth. The NICs are highly trade dependent; trade accounts for between 40 and 150 percent of their GDPs compared to about 15 percent for
Japan and the United States.

The developing countries of East Asia shifted toward export-led
growth paths from earlier import-substitution policies which encouraged development of manufacturing industries by restricting imports of
competing foreign goods—except for Hong Kong and Singapore, where
import-substitution policies were never practical because of the small
size of their internal markets. Exchange rates were adjusted downward
in times of balance of payments deficits, but they tended to be less adjust-
able upward in times of surplus. Import restrictions and exchange rate
misalignments of East Asian NICs have become conspicuous as their
economies have risen in importance and their balance of payments difficulties have become a thing of the past. Although a trade surplus
inevitably causes problems for the surplus country, these are typically in-
sufficient to force it to take up a different set of macroeconomic policies
and to deflect negative political reaction from abroad.

So quicker responses, including steps for wider access for imported
goods and services, currency appreciation, and so forth, must be made.
Most of the East Asian developing countries need to adjust their growth
strategies to emphasize internal sources of growth as opposed to exports.
This does not mean that exports will not be a leading sector in their
economies; it does mean that internal investment and market development should be encouraged alongside exports through deregulation and
liberalization of the domestic economy. Particularly in the ASEAN
countries, there exist many inefficiencies in the domestic economies,
partly the result of government-sanctioned monopolies. In Indonesia,
the Philippines, and Malaysia, there is discussion about privatization
and deregulation, but implementation has lagged far behind the rhetoric.
As direct investments from Trilateral countries in the area mount, the
economic prosperity and political stability of the region will become a
more vital concern for the investor nations; the sense of these countries
"being in the same boat" will be strengthened. The region must maintain
and improve its environment for foreign direct investment.

The growth of manufacturing in the NICs has been encouraged by the
GSP—established more than a decade ago—but the preferences tend to

be monopolized by the more advanced developing countries, while the other East Asian developing countries have benefitted much less. Japan recently made changes in its GSP to help correct this situation. The NICs with chronic trade surpluses should themselves seek to graduate from the GSP, in particular vis-à-vis chronic trade deficit countries.

ASEAN is sufficiently strong and united to take on major roles in the international community. Characterized by loose machinery (the central secretariat building was completed only in 1981), it does not have any rules limiting national sovereignty over policy matters.[17] It offers the best example of regional coalition-building. It should act in more of a leadership role and take more initiative among the countries of the South in international forums.

People's Republic of China

As always, China faces special problems. Through its agricultural and urban reforms, and its open door policy, China has attempted to increase domestic production, invite foreign investment and stimulate exports. These policies, to the extent they can be measured by the growth of the Chinese economy, have been largely successful. China has been dissatisfied, however, by the level of foreign investment and the general tightening of restrictions on high-tech exports due to COCOM.

There is no consensus on China's future economic role in the Asia-Pacific region. At one extreme are those who fear that China will be a massive producer of cheap industrial goods, flooding foreign markets and undercutting other East Asian producers. Others believe that China's recent economic performance represents the one-time effect of the relatively easy liberalization measures it has already taken. This latter group does not expect further dramatic improvements in China's internal economic or export performance unless more fundamental changes are made in Chinese economic and political organization.

It is beyond the scope of this paper to examine the merits and limitations of these arguments. It seems clear, however, that so long as China continues along the path of internal reform, even if slowly, and increases economic contacts with outsiders, Chinese trade with outsiders will grow. For many years, China will have an enormous demand for foreign capital and consumer goods, and for this reason it seems unlikely that China will run large global trade surpluses. Yet it may develop a trade pattern that generates surpluses with North America and Western Europe which pay for imports of capital goods from Japan. China and

---

[17] Tatsumi Okabe, ed., *ASEAN no 20 nen*, "Twenty Years of ASEAN" (Tokyo: Nihon Kokusai Mondai Kenkyusho, December 1987), p. 197.

Japan must take special precautions lest such a pattern create difficult political problems.

China has applied for membership in the GATT, and most GATT members have expressed their support for China's admission. The socialist base of China's economic philosophy, however, raises important and still unresolved questions about the way in which China can carry out its GATT obligations. Still lacking market-determined prices for many commodities and with restrictive import and capital flow practices, China will have to find a means of assuring GATT members that the trade concessions they extend to China through the GATT process will be reciprocated by progressive trade liberalization in China.

Because of China's isolation from the non-Communist countries of the region during most of the postwar period, China's experience with the international trade and monetary system has been relatively limited. The government is training a corps of trade and financial officials, and China's economic laws are still evolving. Labor practices, bureaucracy, and various performance requirements for approval of foreign investment have discouraged foreign businessmen. Many continued domestic adjustments are required before China can become a full member of the international economy.

Conclusion

The East Asian region has prospered without overall intergovernmental machinery (see Appendix B on the Asia-Pacific frameworks that do exist) and is remarkably diverse. While European nations largely share a strong Judeo-Christian heritage, East Asia is devoid of a common spiritual tradition. Spiritual imprints span Buddhism, Islam, Christianity, and Confucianism. The largest country in the region, China, practices its unique version of Communism. Some regimes are repressive; some are permissive. Languages are diverse. Such diversity can be a liability for institution-building, but it can be an asset if it enriches complementarity. And the region is increasingly characterized by economies that are more or less market-oriented and political systems that uphold democratic values.

In this chapter we have stressed the need to adapt global arrangements to accommodate the rise of this diverse region. The global free trade environment and reasonable stability of currencies used for trade are matters of life and death for the region's many economies. At the same time, the region itself needs a regular and effective forum for peer reviews, friendly persuasion, and the building of political will to act together when necessary.

III. The International Environment

The Favorable Balance

The political and economic evolution of East Asia since 1975 has generally favored the interests of the Trilateral countries. The much-feared prospect—seemingly strong in the first three post-war decades—that Communism would spread from China, North Korea, and North Vietnam to much of the rest of the region, has largely evaporated. The end of American military involvement in Indochina in 1975 resulted not in the widely predicted American withdrawal from the region, but instead in a welcome sorting out of priorities. Even though all of Indochina is now under Vietnamese Communist control, in the region as a whole, the influence of radical and anti-Western philosophies has been much reduced. The attraction of Marxist-Leninist doctrines has virtually disappeared, while collectivism as an economic model has lost its credibility even in some Communist countries. The legacy of chaos from the Cultural Revolution remains a powerful reminder of the excesses possible in a Marxist society. The stagnation under Brezhnev similarly shows the inability of Communism to compete economically. The present pathetic state of Indochina under Communist control has lost Hanoi's leaders the respect they once commanded as rebels with a cause.

The trade-oriented development policies of the East Asian market economies have been an important factor in meshing their interests and those of the Trilateral countries. China too, as it seeks to speed its economic modernization, has developed new and important trading and investment links with the Trilateral countries. Roughly half of China's trade in 1986 was with Trilateral countries, and the proportion was higher for some Northeast Asian NICs and ASEAN countries. Trilateral countries are also the primary sources of investment and bilateral aid.[1]

Improved relations and a stronger sense of identity among the countries of the region have also contributed to Trilateral interests in global

---

[1] These links are detailed in Appendix Tables A-6, A-7, A-8 and A-9, and discussed in Chapter II. Among China, the Northeast Asian NICs and the ASEAN 5—nine countries in all—the most typical recent trading pattern is for Japan to be the primary source of imports (8 of 9 in 1986) and the United States the primary destination of exports (5 of 9 in 1986), especially of manufactures.

peace and in the strength and self-reliance of friendly countries. Old divisions among regional states have been significantly modified. ASEAN has taken on major responsibilities for curbing aggression in Southeast Asia and has also become a useful mechanism for strengthening cooperation with other Pacific rim countries and the EC. Australia and New Zealand, accepting the consequences of their geographic position and the growth of the Asian or Pacific sectors of their population, have become predominantly oriented toward the region in which they lie, and play an important regional security role in the adjacent South Pacific. Security links among the non-Communist countries of the region have also multiplied. Such links are not contained within any single institutional framework nor are they likely to become so. They are nevertheless interconnected by the central role of the United States in a web that encompasses its air, naval, and land presence; the military assistance and training it provides to friends and allies; and its security agreements with Japan, South Korea, the Philippines, Thailand, and Australia which, while all bilateral, nevertheless constitute a security umbrella for the region as a whole.

To be sure, overall improvements in relations have not totally eliminated the apprehensions with which the smaller Asian nations regard Japan and China. Particularly in Korea, but elsewhere also, memories of Japanese aggression and exploitation still color attitudes toward Japan, whose present-day economic dominance and policies are also resented. For Southeast Asians, their enormous Chinese neighbor remains a potential if amorphous threat, one that gains an additional dimension in local eyes from the presence throughout Southeast Asia of economically powerful Overseas Chinese minorities. Nevertheless, China and Japan, once rather isolated in the region, are now linked with other East Asian countries and with one another by cooperative ties in many areas. Japan's increased support for South Korea has become an important ingredient of ROK confidence. Its efforts to demonstrate to the ASEAN countries that its concern for their well-being goes beyond its own economic self-interest have also improved the atmosphere. China's opposition to the Vietnamese occupation of Cambodia and its abandonment of several local Communist guerilla movements have strengthened its ties with the ASEAN countries, while its trading relations with other East Asian nations have also grown significantly. While neither China nor Japan can replace the United States in its vital regional defense role, both make contributions to strategic stability that are important in the Atlantic as well as Pacific context.

The regional role of the Soviet Union, beyond its close ties with Vietnam and its now closer relations with North Korea, remains relatively small. Its military expansion in the Pacific has brought it no political advantage; on the contrary, the suspicion with which it is regarded has increased, as has regional support for a continued strong U.S. security role. Its geographic and strategic claims to status as an Asian and Pacific power notwithstanding, its activity and influence are circumscribed by long-standing suspicions of its intentions, more recent antagonism generated by Soviet policies in Indochina and Afghanistan, and, for the market economies, its limited potential as a trading partner. The current Soviet withdrawal from Afghanistan, however, not only meets one of the three Chinese conditions for improved Sino-Soviet relations, but could, over time, add to the pressures on Hanoi for a parallel move in Cambodia.

Conflict and Potential Conflict Areas
Despite a presently more stable security atmosphere in East Asia, the potential for conflict between Communist and non-Communist states persists in the continued confrontations between Vietnam and ASEAN and between the two Koreas, as well as in the still unresolved question of the eventual relationship between Taipei and Beijing.

The struggle in Cambodia no longer seems very likely to ignite broader hostilities in the region. Nevertheless, the disadvantages and dangers of the present situation are not inconsiderable. Incursions into Thailand continue, although on a smaller scale than in earlier years. Hundreds of thousands of Khmer refugees remain displaced along the Thai-Cambodia border. The economic embargo that puts strong pressure on Vietnam to compromise also contributes to the Vietnamese dependence on the USSR that has provided the Soviet Union with a military foothold on Southeast Asian territory for the first time ever. Even as Afghanistan enters a new and more hopeful phase, the much greater tragedy of Cambodia persists, its ability to determine its own future still foreclosed by Vietnamese domination, and the shape that future might take still shadowed by persisting fears of the Khmer Rouge.[2]

In Korea, 37 years have passed since the defeat in 1951 of North Korea's attempt to reunify the peninsula by force. The American commitment to defend the South and the presence of U.S. ground troops to underwrite this pledge constitute an important deterrent to any renewed attempts. Others include the interest of North Korea's Soviet and Chinese allies in continued peace on the peninsula, and the growing strength of South Korea. Nevertheless, the military buildup on both sides of the

---

[2]Hanoi's recent apparent acceptance of a role for Prince Sihanouk is the most encouraging part of the recent flurry of diplomatic activity, but huge gaps separate the contending forces, and, as we go to press, much depends on the next round of Sino-Soviet talks.

DMZ, the opacity of the North Korean policy process, and Pyongyang's terrorism and adventurism weigh heavily against prospects that intermittent North-South dialogue will produce fruitful results any time soon. The continued advantage Pyongyang derives from Seoul's vulnerable proximity to the DMZ, North Korea's high levels of self-sufficiency in military production, its capabilities for surprise attack, and the uncertainties of its succession prospects add further to the explosive potential of continued confrontation on the peninsula.[3]

The situation with respect to Taiwan, by contrast, gives little cause for immediate concern. The economic modernization goals of the PRC constitute a strong compulsion for China remaining on the present course of peaceful attraction, with Hong Kong demonstrating the feasibility of "one country, two systems." Taiwan, for its part, although it continues to maintain and upgrade its defensive capabilities, has become a good deal more relaxed about contacts with the PRC, with over 30,000 Taiwanese already having legally visited the PRC since the relaxation of Taiwan's "no contact" rule. This is an immensely significant change in policy. Still, the present equilibrium remains inherently unstable. Changes in policy on either side of the Straits or a more militant Taiwanese independence movement could still upset today's sense of hope.

Although these dangers and problems persist, they have become localized and less explosive than in earlier years. This is likely to remain the case. Other factors, however, could also affect the present favorable balance of power in East Asia. While the United States remains the prime guarantor of the security of the non-Communist countries of East Asia and the Pacific, its economic ability to continue to carry this burden has declined. At the same time trade differences are spilling over into political relationships in increasingly confrontational ways. The advent of Mikhail Gorbachev and his emphasis on expanding Moscow's role in the region raise further questions.

A New Soviet Union?

Opportunities for the Soviet Union to play a constructive role in the region are numerous: contributing to the reduction of tension on the Korean peninsula; forwarding a resolution of the Cambodian problem; compromising on the Northern Islands; and participating in movement toward arms control agreements in the Pacific. However, while Gorbachev and others have put Soviet dedication to peace in the Pacific in the

---

[3] As this report went to press, in July 1988, President Roh Tae Woo made his imaginative and far-reaching proposals for widespread exchanges between South and North Koreans, and for wider international relationships for both North and South.

forefront of their oratory, Soviet intentions with respect to Vietnam and Korea remain obscure, while the arms proposals advanced so far seem to be primarily directed toward undermining the air and naval capabilities on which American ability to project power in the Pacific depends. Similarly, Soviet pursuit of expanded trade relations with East Asian developing countries, while undoubtedly partly impelled by practical economic considerations, has also been directed toward exploiting trade frictions between the United States and its allies and friends in the region. Relations with China remain the real area of Soviet movement in Asia. Elsewhere in the region, while the exchange of visits has burgeoned and moved to higher levels and trade has increased somewhat, Gorbachev's advent has not yet brought about any basic changes in Soviet posture or in bilateral relations.

The movement toward more normal relations with China, revived in 1982, has indeed accelerated under Gorbachev, reflecting strong interest in promoting the process in Beijing as well as Moscow. The concessions announced at Vladivostok with respect to the Soviet troop presence in Mongolia and the Amur river boundary issue were substantial. One of the two other Chinese conditions for improved Sino-Soviet relations— Soviet withdrawal from Afghanistan—is now being eliminated, though the Vietnamese occupation of Cambodia remains. Economic ties between the two countries have expanded, with the USSR once again providing technical and economic assistance; additional consular offices have been opened in both countries; negotiations over demarcating river boundaries have been reopened after a nine-year lapse; and plans for the joint development of border rivers are under discussion. This progress notwithstanding, the achievement of China's development goals will remain heavily dependent on good relations with the Trilateral countries, while Beijing has not forgotten the discomforts of a close Soviet embrace. The PRC is likely to see its best interests as lying in efforts to fulfill its potential as an important actor on the Asian stage, and in a rough equidistance between the superpowers rather than a genuine alliance with either. Still, Western observers note with special attention that China's new Premier, Li Peng, is Soviet-trained.

Elsewhere in Northeast Asia, the new Gorbachev approach has been more evident in atmospherics than in actual movement. On the crucial issue for Japan—the Northern Islands—Soviet obduracy seems as strong as ever, although it would not be wholly surprising if this legacy of the Gromyko era also changes over time. The inclusion of medium-range missiles based in the Soviet Far East in the recent INF agreement was a welcome step. But, it has not significantly modified Japanese perceptions of the threat posed by the Soviet military buildup in neighboring Asia and the Pacific. Overtures focusing on a major role for Japanese enterprise in the development of Siberia have lost, to declining world markets and prices, the appeal they enjoyed in the '70s.

In recent years, the USSR has reasserted itself as an active player on the Korean stage. Increased Soviet interest in expanding informal ties with South Korea has been strikingly emphasized, and facilitated, by Moscow's decision to participate in the Seoul Olympics. At the same time, the renewed military cooperation between the USSR and North Korea that began with Kim Il Sung's visit to Moscow in May 1984—his first in 17 years—has continued under Gorbachev. It is unlikely that the USSR, in providing Pyongyang with MIG-23s and surface-to-air missiles, has abandoned its interest in the preservation of stability on the peninsula. Rather, its policies toward both North and South probably reflect a mix of new and continuing compulsions: concern about the implications of what it sees as a developing U.S.-Japan-ROK strategic relationship; the pressure to demonstrate support for North Korea to balance what was probably a very early decision that the USSR could not afford to boycott the Seoul Olympics; at the same time, the utility for exerting influence in the North of a demonstrated Soviet capability to move into a new relationship with the South; competition with China for the allegiance of a neighboring Communist state; and interest in strengthening Soviet logistic capabilities and reach in the East Asian area.

In Southeast Asia, it seems clear enough that Moscow welcomes Hanoi's new more flexible tactics. But there is no convincing evidence that Hanoi has altered its position at Moscow's behest. Nor is there yet any reason to believe that interest in improved relations with ASEAN or even China yet extends to the point where the USSR would be prepared to take a stance risking its continued ability to make military use of Vietnamese territory.

Although ASEAN countries have responded to the new Communist flexibility on Cambodia with considerable interest, they are not yet convinced that it will go so far as to permit a settlement on terms they are prepared to accept. Their response to Soviet interest in more active trading and diplomatic relationships has also been somewhat reserved. On the one hand, they welcome new trading opportunities, even relatively marginal ones, and find it desirable also to balance closer ties with China by a somewhat more active relationship with the USSR. On the other hand, Cambodia remains a central issue and long-time suspicions of the USSR are not quickly dispelled. Proposals for cultural and educational exchange are still received more cooly than diplomatic and economic overtures, and Gorbachev's proposals for some new Asian security arrangement have been as massively ignored as Brezhnev's were before him. That a Soviet Foreign Minister has visited Indonesia for the first time in 20 years and Thailand for the first time ever may be a striking manifestation of a new era; but it is also a striking example of how far behind the Trilateral countries the USSR has lagged in developing its diplomatic relations with the ASEAN states.

Whatever the outcome of the Gorbachev approach, the U.S. security commitment and the close alliance between the United States and Japan remain central to the stability of the region. *Disruption of the U.S.-Japan relationship as the result of trade differences would be a disaster of immense proportions.* The burdens imposed by the necessity to maintain a favorable military balance in the Pacific will continue to fall very heavily on American shoulders. U.S.-Philippine base negotiations, however, are creating new uncertainties over the future of the American forward presence while, in any case, budget constraints will have an impact on force levels and deployments. Political and economic realities will thus dictate expanded roles for others—whether in the form of economic contributions to greater regional strength and stability or in direct military expenditures. In the military sphere, burden-sharing has operated mostly in separate and sometimes competing Atlantic and Pacific theatres. More recently, however, common action on Indochina issues and the extension of the INF negotiations to cover weapons deployed in the Soviet Union's Far East as well as in Europe have pointed the way to a more truly Trilateral approach to responsibilities for global security. Economic and, in some cases, military assistance has represented a long-standing European and Canadian contribution to Asia-Pacific security, while Japan is providing significant economic assistance outside its own region.

While military strength must be maintained, it will also be important to seek ways to encourage a constructive Soviet role in the region. Concerted moves toward reducing sources of persisting conflict and tension provide possible opportunities in this regard. Arms control efforts may come to be another. In all such efforts, close consultation and cooperation among Trilateral countries will be indispensable ingredients.

The reduction of tensions between the Soviet Union and the PRC, in that it contributes to the stability of the region as a whole, works to the interests of the Trilateral countries. It is highly unlikely to proceed to a point where a threatening alliance between Beijing and Moscow is reconstituted. While the PRC has its own reasons for preferring equidistance to an overly close relationship with the USSR, it will be important for the Trilateral countries to continue to encourage PRC preoccupation with economic growth.

44

IV. Conclusions and Recommendations

Much has been written in recent years on East Asia's new face, and the foregoing review does not purport to be either conclusive or definitive. Furthermore, each of the three Trilateral areas will, inevitably, look at this vast region from a different vantage point, with different interests, different legacies, and different levels of involvement. (Indeed, further differentiation between individual Trilateral countries will also exist; for example, Canada and the United States look at the region on which they border from considerably different points of view.)

Nonetheless, we believe that it is possible to reach certain general conclusions and recommendations that are relevant to all the Trilateral nations. If these lack at times the specificity that might exist in a single-nation report, this should be regarded as an inevitable consequence of the difference in vantage points. But more importantly, this report, and the degree to which the Trilateral nations can observe issues of such complexity and controversy with a degree of consensus, suggests anew how prescient the original concept of the Trilateral Commission was when it was created in 1973, and how valid and necessary it remains today. The Pacific and Atlantic regions are now inseparable parts of a single global structure, and what happens in one part of the Trilateral world—whether in regard to trade or the strategic balance—has a direct effect on the other parts.

1. *All Trilateral countries must recognize that the keys to overall strategic and political stability in the region remain the U.S. commitment coupled with the U.S.-Japanese relationship.* If at any time the current dangerously high levels of tension between the two nations over trade and other economic issues were to have a fundamental effect on their basic ties, the repercussions would be immense. Every other nation in the region would have to adjust its own policies, and opportunities would be created for adventurism which we believe the Soviets would find it hard to resist. This has been true for over 40 years; we see no likelihood it will change in the remainder of this century.

2. That first conclusion may seem self-evident, even banal, to old Asia hands, who, after all, have been saying such things for many years. But it must be repeated as the first conclusion of any study done in this

American Presidential-election year, because so many Americans, in their understandable frustration at their declining position in the international trading system, have found it increasingly satisfying to lash out against Japan (and South Korea and other East Asian nations) in a manner which might, if unconstrained, ultimately affect the strategic commitments of the United States in the Pacific. To be sure, most American protectionists proclaim that they are not really protectionists at all and that nothing must be done to weaken America's security commitments in the region. But these ritualistic incantations would be worth little if the American public, responding to the red flag of anti-Asian protectionist rhetoric, ended up forgetting why stability in the Pacific was important in the first place.

This is not to conclude that American economic concerns are without foundation. Workers in certain sectors of the American economy have been hurt, and this must be addressed. But the United States—especially in an election year—must remember what it stands for, and how important it remains to all the nations of the Pacific's East Asian rim. It is entirely valid for the United States to call for greater roles for certain other nations in support of common objectives, but the oddly defeatist tone that has colored much of the complaining can only serve to weaken everyone across the entire Trilateral world.

3. If the United States should pull itself back from the brink of the protectionist precipice, then similarly Japan should recognize that with its growing global role comes growing global responsibilities. Tokyo's usual response to calls for greater involvement by Japan in dealing with international problems is, in essence, two-fold: First, Japan is doing much more than it used to; and second, Japan has a unique incremental style, and the rest of the world must understand this and give the country time.

Both arguments have validity, but not enough to justify the slow pace at which Japan is stepping up to its responsibilities. Such statements as Prime Minister Takeshita's December 1987 Manila speech (to the ASEAN summit) represent important steps forward in Japanese thinking. However, the fact remains that in vital areas like ODA levels and contributions to international organizations dealing with the most pressing issues from refugees to basic environmental research, Japan has an opportunity, which we urge it to seize, to change the terrain of the debate dramatically by replacing its traditional incremental approach with a quantum increase in the level of its efforts (as individual Trilateral Commissioners have been recommending for a decade). Such leaps are rare in world affairs, but not without precedent, as the Marshall Plan continually reminds us. A quid pro quo from Washington might make it easier for Japan to take dramatic action. If some such action is not forthcoming, Japan should be prepared for a continuing erosion of positive attitudes towards it over the coming decade.[1]

4. Our focus thus far on Japan and the United States should not be read as overlooking the role of Europe or of Canada. On the contrary, we conclude that the Europeans in particular are still lagging behind where they should be at this time, despite growing trade and awareness of the importance of the region. The situation in East Asia now offers Europe a remarkable opportunity in regard to emerging nations of the region like South Korea, Thailand, and Singapore. Only in regard to China have the Europeans shown deep and sustained interest, attributable partly to the long historic connections, but mainly, we suspect, to a combination of the PRC's sheer size and the aura that it still possesses. Elsewhere in the region, Europe has either failed to keep pace with what is happening, or has viewed East Asia's advance with alarm. In a narrow economic sense this is not surprising, but we believe that the European Community is failing to grasp a real opportunity arising from the desire of the smaller nations of East Asia to reduce their domination by Japan and the United States. Premier Lee Kuan Yew put it well recently: "We desire a still greater presence of the EEC in the region. For in establishing more balanced links with its three principal economic partners—the U.S., Japan, and the EEC—ASEAN would reduce its vulnerability in the event of fluctuations of one or the other of these economies."[2]

There have been some signs of European responses to these interests—as the special adviser to the Thai Premier noted last year—albeit at the elephantine pace so often characteristic of pan-European activity. The EC has had regular ministerial meetings with ASEAN since 1978. These appear to have developed from what one former senior participant characterized as friendly but meaningless encounters into more substantive exchanges. After the October 1986 meeting, Joint Investment Committees were set up in every ASEAN capital; the EC appointed a senior Investment Consultant to liaise between them and European Chambers of Commerce. Eurobankers are showing a keen interest in Thailand in particular. ASEAN is now discussed among European officials in the framework of political cooperation. And the number of ministerial visits to East Asia is on the increase.

---

[1] We applaud the announcement in mid-June that Japan will spend more than $50 billion on ODA from 1988 through 1992. This doubles the amount of aid, in dollar terms, that Japan disbursed over the previous five years, and should raise Japan's ODA/GNP ratio to the DAC average, now 0.35 percent.

[2] Translation from interview with Lee Kuan Yew conducted by François Joyaux and published in French in *Politique Internationale 38* (Winter 1987-88), p. 197.

The moment for more significant initiatives may have arrived. The real prospect of a single Euro-market in 1992, as a result of the agreements reached after much acrimony at the EC's Brussels summit in February 1988, should now concentrate minds on what that great leap forward will mean to dynamic outsiders in East Asia. The thrust of the 1992 program should be toward a more outward-looking and confident Europe, more able to grasp its international opportunities.

Defining a European role in East Asia is even more difficult than detecting it; yet there are propitious circumstances, in addition to local interest. Much of the bitterness associated with the end of empires has disappeared; many of the ties—language, education, friendships— remain, albeit weakened. In another generation, without nurture, they will have disappeared. For instance, it is estimated that 30 percent of Vietnamese children learn French, but that percentage will decline as an aging French-educated elite dies out. Before it is too late, old links should be used to forge new relationships.

Can this slogan be translated into practice? Americans and Japanese smile dismissively, confident of the greater influence of military power and economic muscle. And certainly "new relationships" must include a substantial increase in the willingness of European businessmen to take the investment risks their entrepreneurial forebears assumed in Asia five centuries ago. In those days, state support for the voyagers was a major spur; today, it is even more vital. Only in the context of a politically articulated insistence on the importance of East Asia to Europe's future and a determined diplomatic struggle for fair trading in the area will Europeans look east of Suez again.[3]

The EC Commissioners can and do generate much of the thinking about an increased Euro-role in East Asia; they could do even more by funding a greater intellectual investment in the study of the area. The British Government has set up new university posts for the study of East Asia in the light of the Parker Report's reassessment of the importance of the area, but a bigger, pan-European effort is needed. The EC should increase funding for East Asians to study in Europe and for European scholars to work in East Asia.[4] Educational measures of these types would be key bases for increased Euro-investment in East Asia.

---

[3] To take a concrete example: the entry of South Korea into OECD (proposed in this report) would have to be an opportunity to insist on Seoul's rapid acceptance of the economic responsibilities of its new status. If it were simply an American reward for democratic transformation and a Japanese attempt to improve Seoul-Tokyo relations, it would be regarded cynically and resisted strenuously in Europe.

[4] The communiqué from the May 1988 EC-ASEAN Ministerial Meeting states that "emphasis should be given both to cooperation between universities and other institutions of higher education and to cooperation in the field of sciences in general."

But for the moment, any overarching political dimension can only be provided by national leaders, which in the light of history and status means either the French President or the British Prime Minister, ideally both, and in concert with the German Chancellor. Better still, one of these should take the lead when chairing the European Council.

Even in the absence of a concerted political effort, Europeans can play useful diplomatic roles in East Asia. The United Kingdom maintains strong ties with its Commonwealth partners, Malaysia and Singapore, and its continuing negotiations with the PRC on the basis of the 1984 agreement on the future of Hong Kong constitute an important part of Trilateral engagement with China. The revival of Dutch relations with Indonesia has complemented strong existing West German economic ties there, and makes for a respectable European "presence" in ASEAN's (and OPEC's) largest nation.

France cautiously facilitates the efforts of rival Kampuchean leaders to come to terms; could it not play a more dynamic role without resuscitating fears of neo-colonialism? And if an international conference emerges as the only way to reconcile the many conflicting interests in the area, the United Kingdom, as onetime co-chairman of the Geneva conferences on Indochina, might help take the initiative. In the aftermath of any generally acceptable resolution of the Indochina situation, French expertise (along with Japanese capital) would be important for integrating Vietnam into the world community.

Perhaps even in the Korean peninsula, where the Americans are hampered by politics and the Japanese by history, the less involved Europeans can help explore, in Pyongyang, Beijing, and Moscow, whether North Korea has any interest in desisting from terrorism and ending its intransigent isolation from the non-Communist world.

These kinds of initiatives are likelier to occur if Europeans continue to adopt the more global view of their security concerns symbolized by the despatch of their minesweepers to the Persian Gulf. Equally, East Asians have to emulate the Chinese in appreciating the importance of West European security to their political and economic well-being. East Asians and Europeans have a mutual concern about what Gorbachev's foreign policy implies for security at either end of the Eurasian land mass. Shared perceptions could result in complementary responses. The Western insistence in the early stages of the INF negotiations that any agreement should not result in the redeployment of Soviet missiles from Europe to Asia should be an example not an exception.

All of the above requires more than incremental steps from mid-level and even senior European officials. We believe that it requires, as stated above, a strategic leap of imagination by at least two of Europe's leaders, who would see that by becoming, in effect, supporters of East Asia's emergence in the world, they could bypass Japan and the United States and forge relationships with East Asian leaders who would welcome their friendship. This will not bring overnight results. Decisions and actions should be taken with a view towards playing a major role in the region over the long term.

5. Turning to the issues of political development in East Asia returns us to that most elusive and intangible issue: the linkages between economic growth and political development. There is no simple description of these linkages, which depend on widely varying circumstances in different countries. Nor is there complete agreement about them among the authors of this report. But we do all agree that the next phase of development in East Asia outside of Japan will include this central challenge: Will the political institutions of the region develop and mature to the point where governing systems are stable enough to endure major changes in economic conditions or individual leaders?

The forms that such political development could take vary from nation to nation. We recognize that China is unlikely to develop in the near term in a way which is compatible with the values of Trilateral democracies. Yet there can be little question that China's political system (with little experience with either stability or orderly transitions of power over the last century) has made dramatic progress under Deng Xiaoping. While the true test of that progress will not be passed until three to five years after he leaves the scene, recent events, especially the Thirteenth Party Congress in late 1987, are undeniably impressive steps towards creating a political system which is more predictable and orderly, and more open. Since China remains a Communist state, it is remarkable that any political progress, however limited, has been made there.

Looking beyond China, one finds much to support the view that two decades of economic growth and rising levels of education have created new pressures for broader participation in the political process and that, over time, these pressures have to be met. The most notable case in the last year, of course, has been South Korea.

On the one hand, it could be argued that the historic events in Korea in the last year were the result of accidents: the last-minute conversion of Roh Tae Woo into a democrat; the calming effect of the impending Summer Olympics; the decision of the Army, finally, to stay out of politics; the fortuitous arrival at just the right moment of a strong letter from President Reagan to President Chun Doo Hwan opposing military intervention; and, most importantly, the inability of the opposition leaders to unite behind a single candidate, thus enabling Roh to win the Presidential election with under 40 percent of the vote.

Yet at a deeper level we believe that something more elusive, yet more basic, has been at work. Put most simply, South Koreans are ready for democracy. Finally almost everyone sensed this, and the actions of all the parties concerned were conducted within this new and important limiting perception. The sorts of actions taken as recently as 1980 no longer seem possible to Koreans (or Washington policymakers); Korea has changed in a fundamental way.

The Philippines followed a different route to a similar outcome only a year earlier, and although the Aquino government still faces immense difficulties, its mere survival for over two years, which has defied many predictions, is in itself a major achievement. It is important to note that almost every observer of the Philippine scene agrees that no matter how difficult the situation is today, it would be far worse had Marcos remained in power. How the next transition of power in Manila takes place—whether by election or upheaval—will be crucial to determining the ultimate fate of this unique island nation.

In Taiwan, another strong authoritarian leader's era came to an end in recent months. What is most remarkable and unexpected about this story is that the son of Chiang Kai-Shek turned out to be the man who began the process of reopening the doors between Taiwan and the mainland. It is still far too early to tell what will happen between Beijing and Taipei, or how the internal political situation will evolve in Taiwan. But it is not premature to be hopeful that once again, as with Korea and the Philippines, a new generation of leaders will act to broaden the base of political participation.

Events in Malaysia and Singapore, as discussed earlier, highlight the fact that the movement in the region towards greater popular participation in the political process is not continuous or unified. Malaysia in particular carries the seeds of great racial strife within its bounds, and at present there is a trend towards greater confrontation. And whatever Lee Kuan Yew's justifications, the fact remains that some of his recent actions in regard to political opponents and the press run counter to the values that inspired him and his colleagues in the independence movement. One can only view them with bafflement and sorrow, and hope that they will be temporary.

We accept, indeed embrace, the fact that political development can take many different forms, depending on national characteristics and circumstances. The wide institutional variation among the Trilateral countries underlines the point. It is a misconception that in raising such issues outsiders (particularly Americans) are necessarily trying to replicate in other nations their own forms of government.

The Trilateral nations have a clear and substantial stake in the successful political evolution of the East Asian nations. Without such political evolution, economic progress cannot continue for another two decades as it has over most of the last 20 years. *This is the central challenge for the region over the next decade.* Political structures and institutions must now catch up to the economic achievements of the region, before the cushion afforded by economic growth erodes.

The role and ability of the Trilateral nations in promoting political development in the region varies from country to country. In China, direct outside influence is probably nil, although the impact of outside ideas inside China is undeniable. There are times when outsiders can play an important role in other nations of the region, especially if the limits on outside influence are understood and any involvement is undertaken with extreme care and discretion. This is obviously most true of the United States, which remains the most important external influence on political and strategic events in the region. This influence was exercised effectively during the remarkable events in Manila and Seoul in the last two years, and it is to be hoped that this will continue to be the case.

Other Trilateral nations have lesser roles than the United States, but perhaps larger roles than they themselves realize. If, for example, the EC countries, Japan, and Canada had coordinated their positions in 1985-86 in Manila—they shared a common assessment of the disaster which a continuation of the Marcos regime represented—they might have had an effect on Marcos. Yet with the exception of an ad hoc effort put together by the EC Ambassadors in Manila near the end, we are unaware of any significant actions by the Europeans, Canadians, and Japanese. In regard to other countries, such as Malaysia and Singapore in the current circumstances, we wonder whether, at least at a private level, the United Kingdom in particular could play a role.

There are a variety of indirect roles for Trilateral countries. One of the most important, with the most enduring value, is the provision of educational opportunities in Trilateral universities for students from East Asian developing countries. There is no simple correlation, obviously, between numbers of students educated in Trilateral universities and political liberalization. Yet the education of promising individuals in Trilateral countries is probably an important factor supporting the liberalization process. We applaud the extent to which U.S. and Canadian universities have been open to East Asian students (see Appendix Table A-14). Some 27,000 students from the PRC, it is estimated, are now studying in U.S. universities—and about 22,000 Malaysians. Seoul National University, Beijing University, and Taiwan University have been among the top ten feeder schools in the world into graduate programs at Harvard University.[5] Western European universities have played an important role in this regard as well, most notably in the United Kingdom. The introduction in Britain in 1980 of "full-cost fees" for overseas students stopped the rise in enrollments from developing East Asia, but has been somewhat offset in more recent years by increased assistance for individual students.[6] This is an area of European strength that should be recognized. A much larger role for Japanese universities in educating the region should also be recognized. We hope that current Chinese cutbacks of external educational opportunities in the United States will be only temporary, and fully balanced by greater flows of students to universitites in other Trilateral countries.

Education is only one of several fruitful areas for exchange and cooperation. The importance over time of exchanges of parliamentarians and rising young political leaders, for instance, should not be underestimated. Humanitarian and technical assistance in areas where it is still required can contribute to political as well as economic development. We applaud the emphasis on culture in Prime Minister Takeshita's speech to the December 1987 ASEAN summit in Manila.

6. Trade tensions with the East Asian NICs and other developing East Asian countries are in large measure a consequence of the success of the region in creating the growing prosperity and increasing political stability and maturity which have been important policy goals of the Trilateral countries in the region over time. In responding to the economic challenge, the Trilateral countries should keep in mind their broad goals and responsibilities for international economic management, along with encouraging the NICs to assume larger responsibilities themselves.

The emergence of the East Asian NICs deserves explicit recognition from the Trilateral nations in several specific ways. We recommend a full-scale review of the role of the NICs in leading intergovernmental economic organizations, a review which should also address related issues concerning the role of Japan.

We recommend that the OECD invite the Republic of Korea to join. This process, which cannot be completed overnight, should start in 1988. Regular peer reviews of national policy in a multilateral framework are

---

[5] Seoul National was fourth in 1985-86 and sixth in 1986-87. Beijing was ninth in 1986-87. Taiwan was ninth in 1987-88.

[6] The number of students from ASEAN countries studying in the United Kingdom rose from 1,081 in 1966 to 2,093 in 1970 and 11,829 in 1979. The number then declined, to 7,098 in 1983.

the most important contribution of the OECD to international economic management. Over time, such OECD reviews will help internationally oriented representatives of South Korea gain a sense of policy direction in a framework less politically charged than bilateral interaction with Japan or the United States.

Weighted voting in the IMF and World Bank should be adjusted over the next few years to more fully reflect the increased economic weight of several East Asian countries. Both institutions have struggled with related issues in recent years, but progress has been inadequate.

Under the IMF Articles of Agreement, the Board of Governors is required to conduct general reviews of Fund quotas (to which voting power is tied) at intervals of not more than five years. The Ninth General Review of Quotas in now being negotiated (and has been delayed beyond the five-year mark of March 31, 1988). The quota of Japan should be significantly increased. As Appendix Table A-10 indicates, Japan remains behind France, West Germany, and the United Kingdom after the Eighth General Review. Among other East Asian countries the most obvious case of an excessively small quota is South Korea, which was at the same level as New Zealand after the Eighth Review.[7]

The World Bank has already made the transition to a larger shareholding for Japan than for any single West European country (see Appendix Table A-11), but the Japanese share remains low relative to the size of the Japanese economy. The General Capital Increase (GCI) anounced in February 1988 does not change the relative size of authorized shareholdings. Relative increases for some other economies in East Asia were an important point in dispute during negotiations on the new GCI. Rather than hold up the GCI, this issue (tied to voting shares) was postponed and a task force set up to report to the Bank's Governors this fall.

Along with enlarged voting power, Japan in particular should expect its nationals to occupy a larger portion of senior positions in the Bank and Fund. Japanese candidates should be given serious consideration when the choice is next made of a World Bank President or IMF Managing Director. We encourage the Japanese government to become more active on policy issues in the Bank and Fund. We applaud the relatively large financial participation of Japan in IDA (International Development Association) and special facilities, and believe it should be further enlarged.

The relationship of other rapidly developing countries of East Asia to the Fund and Bank should change over time. An important indicator of

---

[7] The Eighth Review specified a quota for Singapore of 250.2 million SDRs, but as of April 30, 1987 (see Appendix Table A-10), Singapore had not consented to this increase and remained at 92.4 million SDRs. After the Sixth Review (in the 1970s), Singapore consented to an increase less than the full amount specified by the Fund's Board of Governors.

acceptance of broader responsibilities in the international economy is acceptance of IMF Article VIII obligations. The United States accepted these obligations in 1946 and Canada in 1952. Most West European countries took this step in 1961; Japan did so in 1964 (the same year it joined the OECD). Among the East Asian NICs and ASEAN countries, only Malaysia and Singapore have taken this step (both in 1968), while Hong Kong is covered by British acceptance until 1997. It is time for South Korea to take this step, and for Taiwan—although not an IMF member—to recognize these obligations anyway.

The 1982 World Bank Annual Report noted that the "graduation of borrowers from the IBRD is a firmly established principle and has been a long-standing practice." The Executive Directors that year established guidelines—"Graduation will normally occur within five years after a country reaches the per capita gross national product (GNP) benchmark of $2,650 at 1980 prices"—though the guidelines have not been rigidly applied over time. Singapore has received no new IBRD loans in this decade, though this is apparently due less to "graduation" than to the availability of more attractive borrowing arrangements elsewhere. South Korea, one of the World Bank's largest borrowers over time,[8] is now borrowing much less. The ROK has participated as a donor since the Sixth Replenishment of IDA resources.

7. Strategic considerations in East Asia and the Pacific have received somewhat less attention in recent years from Trilateral governments (though not from the Trilateral Commission, as the 1985 Nishihara report demonstrates[9]). The threats to stability have seemed greater elsewhere, and we have seen a period of relative strategic stability in the region. Sino-Soviet tensions are down markedly (but still exist). Only in the Philippines and Burma are guerilla struggles still threatening. There is progress between Taiwan and the mainland. The Vietnamese are looking for ways to lower tensions in Cambodia, although the price they are prepared to pay remains uncertain. Some discern signs of change in North Korea. But none of these particular problems is close to ultimate resolution, and each still contains the seeds of a return to an instability that would be costly to the entire region.

8. As with the Tokyo-Washington relationship, there is a tendency now to take for granted that the course of the People's Republic of China will remain that of a stable and peaceful participant in the region's affairs. But

---

[8] As of June 30, 1987, South Korea was the sixth largest cumulative borrower from the IBRD (after Brazil, India, Mexico, Indonesia, and Turkey).

[9] Masashi Nishihara, *East Asian Security and the Trilateral Countries.*

such complacency is hardly justified, even though the relationships of the Trilateral countries with the People's Republic have improved enormously since the end of the Cultural Revolution a decade ago. While it was under Mao, as a result of Sino-Soviet tension, that breakthroughs to better relations occurred with Western Europe, Japan, Canada, and even the "imperialist" United States, it has been the post-Mao reform program of Deng Xiaoping that has opened up China to the industrialized democracies.

China's "new deal" has meant greater prosperity for the majority of the population which lives in the countryside. Though campaigns against "spiritual pollution" and "bourgeois liberalization" and the hounding of some leading writers and academics have shown that the Chinese leadership will still maintain boundaries which must not be crossed, there is nevertheless a greater readiness to allow a "hundred flowers" to bloom in the intellectual sphere. Undoubtedly, this is the most hopeful period in the 40-year history of the PRC in terms of both peace abroad and development at home.

Yet it has to be recognized that certain Chinese domestic issues and international concerns may sour this generally positive picture. While reformers led by General Secretary Zhao Ziyang are currently in the ascendant, bureaucratic opposition, urban disquiet, and real difficulties are sufficient to make the future course of the reform program uncertain. The test will not come until after Deng finally passes from the scene. If thereafter China less vigorously promotes peasant entrepreneurship and managerial autonomy, the open door to the businessmen of the industrial democracies will not be so widely ajar. And if another leadership struggle erupts, as is always possible, the effect on economic cooperation with outsiders could be immediate—to say nothing of the consequences for China itself.

Internationally, China is seeking a role less beholden to either of the superpowers, something more like equidistance between Washington and Moscow, without sacrificing the enormous advantages of good relations with the United States. This realignment will be spurred if those advantages have to be reassessed. Already, as noted above, Beijing has decided to cut back heavily on the number of students who will be allowed to go the the United States because of the high percentage of the first wave who are expected not to come home, though more will be sent elsewhere in the Trilateral areas. Problems over technology transfer, declining corporate interest in investing in the PRC, Congressional concern over Chinese weapons sales or Tibet or human rights in general, and miscalculated moves on Taiwan are the kinds of issues which could sour the Sino-American relationship.

Under such circumstances, it would be particularly important for other nations of the Trilateral world to maintain their generally less emotion-ridden friendship with the PRC. Indeed, the continuing engagement of the industrialized democracies with a rapidly developing China is so vital to the security of East Asia that it should be made a matter of regular Trilateral consultation.

9. Finally, let us turn again to the challenge from the Soviet Union. It is understandable that the Soviet Union would view itself as a Pacific power: geography, military forces, history, and a sense of destiny all give the Soviets reason to consider themselves an important part of the region. But a vital question remains unresolved in the Gorbachev era: what *kind* of Pacific power—disruptive or cooperative, expansionary or willing to accept the status quo, encouraging Hanoi's aggressiveness or restraining it?

So far, the remarkable changes in Soviet behavior in regard to so many issues, both internal and external, do not seem to have reached East Asia. With the exception of a noticeable reduction in tensions between Moscow and Beijing, little has changed in the region. Gorbachev's 1986 Vladivostok speech attracted international attention, but it is still not clear, two years later, exactly what he meant. Moscow's statements on Cambodia, where it could play a significant role, continue generally to echo Hanoi's. There has been no change in the Soviet position on the Northern Islands, and without such a change there is little prospect of a major improvement in Soviet-Japanese relations.

Above all, the nations of the region still do not know whether the Soviet Union, under Gorbachev, will follow a disruptive or a cooperative road in developing its Pacific and East Asian presence. In the early 1970s, Moscow embarked upon a significant buildup of its naval forces and bases in the region, culminating in its presence at Cam Ranh Bay. The buildup has more recently levelled off, but we do not know if this is because the Soviet presence reached the levels originally sought by Moscow, or if the Soviets simply decided that additional military capabilities would create a unifying anti-Soviet backlash in the region.

Perhaps Moscow itself has not yet decided which course to take. Opportunism, after all, is based on opportunity. The authors of this report believe strongly that more should be made of the importance of East Asia and the Pacific in high-level dialogue with Moscow, lest the Soviets underestimate the region's importance to the United States and other Trilateral countries. Such a conclusion on Moscow's part could lead it into adventures to which the United States (hopefully supported by other Trilateral nations) would have no alternative but to respond. We urge the leaders of all the Trilateral nations to make clear to the Soviet Union that they attach equal importance to the Atlantic and Pacific regions. If Moscow seeks to change the present strategic or political balance, it should be clearly on notice that the Trilateral countries will respond.

* * *

The enormous achievements in East Asia in the last two decades have been celebrated, or viewed with alarm, by the whole world in recent years. They are among the most important new facts of the last decades of the Twentieth Century. The much-heralded Pacific Century may well be upon us already—but only if the political process catches up with the economic process in the region. The big news from East Asia in the last two years—from the Philippines, Korea, Taiwan, and China—may be that this process is finally underway. But equally big question marks remain. The Trilateral countries must watch, and be prepared to play significant supporting roles.

APPENDIX A: SUPPORTING TABLES

Economic Growth

Table 2 in the main text provided 1986 GNP and GNP per capita levels for East Asian countries, and compared them to similar indicators for Trilateral countries. Table A-1 below shows changes over time between 1973 and 1986. The real growth of GNP per capita in much of East Asia was particularly impressive. With the notable exception of the Philippines, the ASEAN countries grew more than twice as fast (in real per capita GNP terms) as the global average for middle-income countries, and the NICs grew roughly four times as fast as that average. The Chinese rate was among the highest in the region. The Japanese rate was almost twice the average for industrial market economies. Over time such differentials in growth rates have a major impact on relative levels.

TABLE A-1
Real Growth Rates, 1973-86
(percent)

	GNP	GNP per capita
Japan	4.3	3.4
China	7.4	5.9
Northeast Asian NICs		
South Korea	7.2	5.6
Taiwan	8.1	6.2
Hong Kong	8.5	6.1
ASEAN		
Indonesia	6.1	3.8
Philippines	3.3	0.6
Thailand	5.9	3.5
Malaysia	6.3	3.8
Singapore	7.6	6.3
Low-income countries	*3.6*	*0.8*
(except China and India)		
Middle-income countries	*3.9*	*1.5*
High-income oil exporters	*5.5*	*0.3*
Industrial market economies	*2.5*	*1.8*

Sources: International Economics Department, World Bank, *Recent Economic and Social Indicators* (Washington, D.C.: September 1987), pp. 4-5 (except Taiwan); Council for Economic Planning and Development, Republic of China, *Taiwan Statistical Data Book 1987* (Taipei: June 1987), p. 2.

Leading Exporters

The rise of the East Asian NICs is quite evident in the listing below of the world's leading exporting countries. Note the rise in rank between 1973 and 1986 of Taiwan, Hong Kong, South Korea and Singapore. The share of China has risen by half. The share of Japan has also risen substantially, though its ranking remained the same in 1986 as in 1973. The shares of these countries are larger (except for Singapore and China) when we restrict our view to exports of manufactures, as in Table A-3.

TABLE A-2
**The 25 Leading Exporters in
World Merchandise Trade in 1986**

Rank			Share (percent)	
1973	1986		1973	1986
2	1	Federal Republic of Germany	11.8	11.5
1	2	United States	12.5	10.5
3	*3*	*Japan*	*6.4*	*9.9*
4	4	France	6.3	5.9
5	5	United Kingdom	5.2	5.0
9	6	Italy	3.9	4.6
10	8	USSR	3.7	4.6
6	8	Canada	4.4	4.2
7	9	Netherlands	4.2	3.8
8	10	Belgium-Luxembourg	3.9	3.2
27	*11*	*Taiwan*	*0.8*	*1.9*
12	12	Switzerland	1.7	1.8
11	13	Sweden	2.1	2.1
24	*14*	*Hong Kong*	*0.9*	*1.7*
39	*15*	*South Korea*	*0.6*	*1.6*
20	*16*	*China*	*1.0*	*1.5*
23	17	Spain	0.9	1.3
16	18	German Democratic Republic	1.3	1.2
14	19	Saudi Arabia	1.6	1.1
13	20	Australia	1.6	1.1
33	*21*	*Singapore*	*0.6*	*1.1*
22	22	Austria	0.9	1.1
17	23	Brazil	1.1	1.1
19	24	Denmark	1.1	1.1
21	25	Czechoslovakia	1.0	1.0

Sources: GATT, *International Trade 1985-86* (Geneva. 1986), pp. 23 24, and *International Trade 1986-87* (Geneva: 1987), p. 156.

TABLE A-3
**The 25 Leading Exporters
of Manufactures in 1986**

Rank 1986		Share (percent)				
		1970	1973	1980	1985	1986
1	Federal Republic of Germany	15.7	17.0	14.8	13.3	14.9
2	*Japan*	*9.4*	*9.9*	*11.2*	*14.2*	*14.1*
3	United States	14.9	12.6	12.7	12.1	10.3
4	France	6.9	7.3	7.4	6.0	6.3
5	Italy	5.7	5.3	6.0	5.6	6.0
6	United Kingdom	8.1	7.0	7.5	5.5	5.4
7	Canada	4.3	3.5	2.8	4.3	3.7
8	Belgium-Luxembourg	4.5	4.9	4.1	3.2	3.5
9	Netherlands	3.5	3.9	3.4	2.9	3.2
10	*Taiwan*	*0.6*	*1.1*	*1.6*	*2.3*	*2.5*
11	Switzerland	2.4	2.4	2.4	2.1	2.4
12	*Hong Kong*	*1.2*	*1.3*	*1.6*	*2.3*	*2.5*
13	*South Korea*	*0.3*	*0.8*	*1.4*	*2.3*	*2.2*
14	USSR	2.6	2.2	1.8	1.7	1.7
15	Sweden	2.7	2.6	2.2	2.0	2.2
16	German Democratic Republic	1.9	1.7	1.2	1.5	-
17	Spain	0.7	0.9	1.4	1.4	1.4
18	Czechoslovakia	1.5	1.3	1.6	1.3	-
19	Austria	1.2	1.2	1.3	1.2	1.4
20	*China*	*0.2*	*0.2*	*0.3*	*0.8*	*1.0*
21	*Singapore*	*0.2*	*0.5*	*0.8*	*1.0*	*0.9*
22	Finland	0.8	0.8	0.9	0.9	0.9
23	Denmark	0.9	1.0	0.8	0.8	0.9
24	Brazil	0.2	0.3	0.7	1.3	0.8
25	Hungary	0.8	0.9	0.7	0.7	0.7

Source: GATT, *International Trade 1986-87*, p. 194.

Health and Education Improvements

The progress of much of East Asia is also evident in various societal indicators, as Tables A-4 and A-5 show.

TABLE A-4
Life Expectancy and Infant Mortality Rates

| | Life Expectancy[1] | | | | Infant Mortality[2] | |
| | Male | | Female | | | |
	1965	1985	1965	1985	1965	1985
Japan	68	75	73	80	18	6
China	54	68	55	70	90	35
Northeast Asian NICs						
South Korea	55	65	58	72	63	27
Taiwan	65	71	70	76	24	7
Hong Kong	64	73	71	79	28	9
ASEAN						
Indonesia	43	53	45	57	138	96
Philippines	54	61	57	65	72	48
Thailand	54	62	58	66	88	43
Malaysia	56	66	60	70	55	28
Singapore	64	70	68	75	26	9
Brunei	n.a.	n.a.	n.a.	n.a.	n.a.	n.a.
Indochina						
Vietnam	48	63	51	67	n.a.	49
Kampuchea	43	n.a.	46	n.a.	134	n.a.
Laos	n.a.	44	n.a.	46	n.a.	151
Burma	46	57	49	61	122	66
North Korea	55	65	58	71	63	27
Low-income countries (except China and India)	*44*	*51*	*45*	*53*	*150*	*112*
Middle-income countries	*53*	*60*	*56*	*64*	*104*	*68*
High-income oil exporters	*48*	*61*	*51*	*65*	*115*	*61*
Industrial market countries	*68*	*73*	*74*	*79*	*23*	*9*

Sources: World Bank, *World Development Report 1987* (New York: Oxford University Press, 1987), pp. 258-59 (except Taiwan); Directorate-General of Budget, Accounting and Statistics, Executive Yuan, The Republic of China, *Statistical Yearbook of the Republic of China 1987*, Table 19, p. 3.

[1] at birth, in years
[2] deaths of infants aged under one year per thousand live births in a given year

TABLE A-5
Education
(number enrolled in school as percent of age group)

	Primary[1]		Secondary		Higher Education	
	1965	1984	1965	1984	1965	1984
Japan	100	100	82	95	13	30
China	89	110	24	37	(.)	1
Northeast Asian NICs						
South Korea	101	99	35	91	6	26
Taiwan	97	100	38	89	7	13
Hong Kong	103	105	29	69	5	13
ASEAN						
Indonesia	72	118	12	39	1	7
Philippines	113	107	41	68	19	29
Thailand	78	97	14	30	2	23
Malaysia	90	97	28	53	2	6
Singapore	105	115	45	71	10	12
Brunei						
Indochina						
Vietnam	n.a.	113	n.a.	48	n.a.	n.a.
Kampuchea	77	n.a.	9	n.a.	1	n.a.
Laos	40	90	2	19	(.)	1
Burma	71	102	15	24	1	5
North Korea	n.a.	n.a.	n.a.	n.a.	n.a.	n.a.
Low-income countries (except China and India)	*44*	*70*	*9*	*23*	*1*	*3*
Middle-income countries	*85*	*104*	*22*	*47*	*6*	*13*
High-income oil exporters	*43*	*75*	*10*	*45*	*1*	*10*
Industrial market economies	*107*	*102*	*63*	*90*	*21*	*38*

Sources: World Bank, *World Development Report 1987*, pp. 262-63 (except Taiwan); *Statistical Yearbook of the Republic of China 1987*, Supplemental Table 7, p. 249

[1] For some countries, the gross enrollment ratios may exceed 100 percent because some pupils are younger or older than the country's standard primary school age.

Trade with Trilateral Countries

Table A-6 indicates Trilateral shares in the trade of China, the Northeast Asian NICs, and the ASEAN countries. Japan tends to be the leading source of imports. In contrast, the United States is the leading destination for exports, except for China, Indonesia, Thailand and Malaysia. Table A-6 also indicates that the EC countries as a whole have a major trading presence in the region. In 1986, EC countries together were a larger trading partner (exports plus imports) than the United States of China and Thailand, and a larger supplier of exports to Indonesia and Hong Kong. Canada, with a population about one-tenth of the United States, has a trading presence in the region that is roughly proportionate (stronger in China, weaker in some other countries). Table A-7 provides bilateral trade balances, and indicates many important changes between 1980 and 1986. (Complete 1987 figures were not available before publication of this report.)

TABLE A-6

Exports and Imports of East Asian Developing Countries: Trilateral Shares
(percent)

China

	1980		1982		1984		1985		1986	
	Exp	Imp	Exp	Imp	Exp	Imp	Exp	Imp	Exp	Imp
Japan	22.3	26.5	21.9	20.6	20.8	31.0	22.3	35.7	15.1	28.7
Canada	0.8	4.2	0.8	6.6	1.0	4.1	0.9	2.7	1.0	2.3
USA	5.4	19.6	8.1	22.8	9.3	14.8	8.6	12.2	8.4	10.8
EC	13.1	14.4	9.9	11.5	9.0	12.8	8.4	14.5	12.8	17.8
France	*1.9*	*1.6*	*1.3*	*1.2*	*0.9*	*1.4*	*0.8*	*1.7*	*1.0*	*1.7*
FRG	*3.9*	*6.8*	*3.5*	*5.1*	*3.1*	*4.8*	*2.7*	*5.8*	*3.2*	*8.4*
UK	*3.1*	*2.8*	*1.4*	*1.4*	*1.3*	*2.0*	*1.3*	*1.8*	*4.6*	*2.3*
Italy	*1.9*	*1.3*	*1.1*	*1.7*	*1.2*	*1.7*	*1.1*	*2.1*	*1.2*	*2.6*
Neth.	*1.1*	*0.8*	*1.3*	*0.5*	*1.3*	*0.6*	*1.2*	*0.6*	*1.5*	*0.6*
World Total (billion $US)	$18.1	$19.5	$21.9	$18.9	$24.8	$26.0	$27.3	$42.5	$31.4	$43.5

TABLE A-6 (continued)
Exports and Imports of East Asian Developing Countries: Trilateral Shares
(percent)

South Korea

	1980		1982		1984		1985		1986 est.	
	Exp	Imp	Exp	Imp	Exp	Imp	Exp	Imp	Exp	Imp
Japan	17.4	26.3	15.6	21.9	15.8	24.9	15.5	25.3	15.2	33.0
Canada	2.0	1.7	2.0	2.0	3.0	2.1	4.1	2.0	3.4	2.1
USA	26.4	21.9	28.8	24.6	36.0	22.5	36.2	21.5	38.5	20.2
EC	15.6	7.3	13.3	7.2	11.3	9.1	10.7	9.6	12.5	10.8
France	*1.7*	*0.9*	*1.2*	*0.9*	*1.0*	*1.1*	*1.0*	*1.4*	*1.7*	*2.3*
FRG	*5.0*	*2.9*	*3.5*	*2.8*	*3.2*	*2.6*	*3.0*	*2.9*	*3.4*	*4.0*
UK	*3.3*	*1.4*	*4.7*	*1.7*	*3.3*	*1.8*	*3.0*	*1.7*	*3.0*	*1.6*
Italy	*1.3*	*0.5*	*0.7*	*0.5*	*0.6*	*0.7*	*0.6*	*0.8*	*0.8*	*1.0*
Neth.	*2.0*	*0.4*	*1.6*	*0.5*	*1.3*	*1.0*	*1.0*	*0.8*	*1.4*	*0.6*
World Total (billion $US)	$17.4	$22.1	$21.8	$24.3	$29.3	$30.6	$30.3	$31.1	$35.6	$33.3

Taiwan

	1980		1982		1984		1985		1986 est.	
	Exp	Imp	Exp	Imp	Exp	Imp	Exp	Imp	Exp	Imp
Japan	11.0	27.1	10.7	25.3	10.5	29.3	11.3	27.6	11.4	34.2
Canada	2.3	1.3	2.3	1.7	3.0	1.8	3.1	1.8	3.2	2.0
USA	34.1	23.7	39.4	24.1	48.8	23.0	48.1	23.6	47.7	22.4
EC	15.8	9.5	11.7	11.2	10.0	10.8	9.8	12.2	n.a.	n.a.
France	*1.4*	*0.6*	*1.1*	*1.7*	*0.8*	*1.0*	*0.7*	*1.3*	*n.a.*	*n.a.*
FRG	*5.4*	*3.7*	*3.5*	*4.2*	*2.9*	*3.5*	*2.6*	*4.2*	*3.2*	*4.7*
UK	*2.4*	*1.5*	*2.4*	*1.4*	*2.3*	*1.3*	*2.1*	*1.3*	*2.4*	*1.5*
Italy	*1.5*	*0.8*	*0.9*	*1.0*	*0.7*	*1.0*	*0.8*	*1.2*	*n.a.*	*n.a.*
Neth.	*2.3*	*0.9*	*1.5*	*0.8*	*1.4*	*1.1*	*1.5*	*1.1*	*1.7*	*n.a.*
World Total (billion $US)	$19.8	$19.7	$22.2	$18.9	$30.5	$21.9	$30.7	$20.1	$39.8	$24.2

TABLE A-6 (continued)
Exports and Imports of East Asian Developing Countries: Trilateral Shares
(percent)

Hong Kong

	1978		1982		1984		1985		1986	
	Exp	Imp	Exp	Imp	Exp	Imp	Exp	Imp	Exp	Imp
Japan	7.7	22.8	4.5	22.1	4.4	23.6	4.2	23.1	4.7	20.4
Canada	--	--	2.3	0.8	2.8	0.7	2.4	0.7	2.4	0.5
USA	30.4	11.9	28.9	10.8	33.2	10.9	30.8	9.5	31.4	8.4
EC	21.8	14.2	17.7	12.2	14.0	10.9	12.3	11.5	14.5	11.5
France	*1.2*	*1.7*	*1.4*	*1.4*	*1.1*	*1.4*	*1.0*	*1.3*	*1.3*	*1.3*
FRG	*8.6*	*3.3*	*6.1*	*2.5*	*4.8*	*2.5*	*4.1*	*2.9*	*5.0*	*2.9*
UK	*7.4*	*4.7*	*6.2*	*4.8*	*5.2*	*3.9*	*4.2*	*3.6*	*4.5*	*3.4*
Italy	*0.9*	*1.5*	*0.9*	*1.4*	*0.7*	*1.3*	*0.7*	*1.5*	*0.9*	*1.6*
Neth.	*1.9*	*1.0*	*1.5*	*0.6*	*1.3*	*0.7*	*1.1*	*0.7*	*1.3*	*0.7*
China	0.5	16.7	8.9	21.3	17.8	25.0	26.0	25.5	21.3	29.6
(reexports)			(6.3)		(12.7)		(n.a.)			
(imports for reexport)				(10.2)		(n.a.)		(n.a.)		
World Total (billion $US)			$20.9	$23.4	$21.9	$24.0	$30.2	$29.7	$35.4	$35.4

Indonesia

	1980		1982		1984		1985		1986	
	Exp	Imp	Exp	Imp	Exp	Imp	Exp	Imp	Exp	Imp
Japan	49.3	31.5	50.1	25.4	47.3	23.8	49.1	28.1	44.9	29.2
Canada	0.1	0.9	0.1	0.8	0.2	2.3	0.2	2.0	0.4	2.0
USA	19.6	13.0	15.9	14.3	20.6	18.4	22.7	14.4	19.6	13.9
EC	6.5	13.6	4.1	16.3	5.0	15.4	6.2	18.3	9.3	17.2
France	*0.6*	*2.2*	*0.3*	*3.4*	*0.2*	*3.1*	*0.7*	*4.2*	*0.6*	*2.6*
FRG	*1.8*	*6.3*	*1.1*	*7.1*	*1.1*	*5.9*	*1.6*	*7.9*	*2.3*	*6.7*
UK	*0.6*	*2.4*	*0.6*	*2.6*	*0.8*	*2.1*	*1.0*	*3.4*	*1.3*	*3.2*
Italy	*1.2*	*0.7*	*0.6*	*0.6*	*0.8*	*0.8*	*1.0*	*1.4*	*1.0*	*1.3*
Neth.	*1.9*	*1.1*	*1.2*	*1.1*	*1.5*	*1.9*	*1.7*	*2.3*	*3.1*	*1.8*
World Total (billion $US)	$21.9	$10.8	$22.3	$16.9	$21.9	$13.9	$18.6	$10.2	$14.8	$10.7

TABLE A-6 (continued)
Exports and Imports of East Asian Developing Countries: Trilateral Shares
(percent)

Philippines

	1980 Exp	1980 Imp	1982 Exp	1982 Imp	1984 Exp	1984 Imp	1985 Exp	1985 Imp	1986 Exp	1986 Imp
Japan	26.6	19.9	22.9	20.1	19.4	13.6	19.0	14.0	17.7	17.1
Canada	1.1	1.0	1.2	1.0	1.5	0.8	1.6	0.7	1.4	0.9
USA	27.5	23.5	31.6	22.5	38.0	27.4	35.9	25.1	35.6	24.9
EC	17.5	10.7	15.1	11.3	14.0	10.9	14.1	8.4	18.3	11.0
France	*1.6*	*1.1*	*1.6*	*1.3*	*1.8*	*2.2*	*1.9*	*1.4*	*2.3*	*1.5*
FRG	*4.4*	*4.2*	*4.0*	*4.3*	*3.3*	*3.2*	*3.8*	*2.8*	*5.0*	*4.2*
UK	*2.5*	*2.3*	*3.8*	*2.1*	*4.2*	*2.4*	*3.6*	*2.0*	*4.8*	*2.1*
Italy	*1.1*	*0.8*	*0.7*	*0.6*	*0.5*	*0.4*	*0.6*	*0.6*	*0.5*	*0.5*
Neth.	*6.3*	*1.4*	*3.8*	*1.1*	*3.1*	*0.9*	*3.1*	*0.8*	*4.5*	*1.4*
World Total (billion $US)	$5.8	$8.3	$5.0	$8.3	$5.3	$6.3	$4.6	$5.4	$4.8	$5.2

Thailand

	1980 Exp	1980 Imp	1982 Exp	1982 Imp	1984 Exp	1984 Imp	1985 Exp	1985 Imp	1986 est. Exp	1986 est. Imp
Japan	15.1	21.2	13.7	23.5	13.0	26.9	13.3	26.0	14.0	26.2
Canada	0.4	1.4	0.4	1.4	1.2	1.2	1.2	1.2	1.4	1.3
USA	12.7	14.5	12.7	13.4	17.2	13.5	19.6	11.2	17.9	13.7
EC	26.0	13.4	23.7	11.9	20.7	12.4	19.1	14.7	21.4	15.9
France	*1.6*	*1.0*	*1.9*	*1.5*	*1.7*	*1.6*	*1.8*	*4.5*	*2.3*	*2.4*
FRG	*4.1*	*4.4*	*3.4*	*3.9*	*3.3*	*4.2*	*3.7*	*5.2*	*4.6*	*5.7*
UK	*1.9*	*2.7*	*1.9*	*2.6*	*2.2*	*2.3*	*2.4*	*2.6*	*3.2*	*3.1*
Italy	*2.0*	*1.4*	*1.6*	*1.1*	*1.7*	*1.2*	*1.7*	*1.1*	*1.7*	*1.1*
Neth.	*13.2*	*2.5*	*13.2*	*1.2*	*10.0*	*1.1*	*7.1*	*1.0*	*7.3*	*1.2*
World Total (billion $US)	$6.5	$9.2	$6.9	$8.5	$7.4	$10.4	$7.1	$9.3	$8.8	$9.3

TABLE A-6 (continued)
Exports and Imports of East Asian Developing Countries: Trilateral Shares
(percent)

Malaysia

	1980		1982		1984		1985		1986	
	Exp	Imp	Exp	Imp	Exp	Imp	Exp	Imp	Exp	Imp
Japan	22.8	22.8	20.3	25.0	22.8	26.3	24.6	23.0	22.6	20.6
Canada	0.5	1.1	0.5	1.2	0.8	0.9	0.7	1.2	0.8	1.2
USA	16.4	15.1	11.6	17.6	13.5	16.3	12.8	15.3	16.6	18.8
EC	17.5	15.8	15.4	12.4	13.0	13.7	14.4	14.4	14.7	14.7
France	*1.8*	*1.9*	*1.2*	*1.3*	*0.9*	*2.4*	*1.1*	*2.3*	*1.4*	*2.1*
FRG	*3.6*	*5.4*	*2.8*	*4.2*	*3.0*	*4.2*	*2.6*	*4.5*	*3.6*	*4.5*
UK	*2.8*	*5.4*	*2.7*	*4.1*	*2.5*	*3.6*	*2.6*	*4.0*	*3.5*	*4.6*
Italy	*1.6*	*1.2*	*0.9*	*1.0*	*0.9*	*1.2*	*0.8*	*1.2*	*0.9*	*1.3*
Neth.	*6.0*	*0.6*	*6.0*	*0.7*	*4.0*	*1.0*	*5.8*	*1.1*	*3.4*	*0.9*
World Total (billion $US)	$13.0	$10.8	$12.0	$12.4	$16.6	$14.1	$15.4	$12.3	$13.8	$10.8

Singapore

	1980		1982		1984		1985		1986	
	Exp	Imp	Exp	Imp	Exp	Imp	Exp	Imp	Exp	Imp
Japan	8.1	18.0	10.9	17.9	9.4	18.4	9.4	17.1	8.6	19.9
Canada	0.7	0.5	0.6	0.4	0.8	0.5	0.7	0.3	0.7	0.4
USA	12.5	14.1	12.6	12.9	20.0	14.6	21.2	15.2	23.4	15.0
EC	12.8	11.2	9.7	10.5	10.1	10.3	10.6	11.3	11.1	11.7
France	*2.2*	*1.4*	*1.5*	*1.9*	*1.2*	*1.7*	*1.5*	*2.3*	*1.5*	*1.7*
FRG	*3.0*	*3.3*	*2.2*	*3.2*	*2.4*	*2.7*	*2.2*	*2.7*	*3.1*	*3.3*
UK	*2.6*	*3.4*	*2.0*	*2.8*	*2.7*	*2.6*	*2.7*	*2.9*	*2.6*	*3.4*
Italy	*1.3*	*0.9*	*0.8*	*1.0*	*1.0*	*1.5*	*1.1*	*1.4*	*1.0*	*1.3*
Neth.	*1.9*	*1.3*	*1.7*	*0.7*	*1.2*	*0.8*	*1.3*	*1.0*	*1.5*	*0.9*
World Total (billion $US)	$19.4	$24.0	$20.8	$28.2	$24.1	$28.7	$22.8	$26.2	$22.5	$25.5

Sources: IMF, *Direction of Trade Statistics Yearbook 1987* (Washington: 1987), various tables; and Jacques Machizaud, *Le Role de la France dans le Pacifique Nord*, Conseil Economique et Social 596/SG/54 (Paris: 1986), various tables. The 1986 Taiwan figures are from *Taiwan Statistical Data Book 1987*, pp. 215-19; and *Statistical Yearbook of the Republic of China 1987*, pp. 384-87.

TABLE A-7
Bilateral Trade Balances of Trilateral Countries with East Asian Developing Countries, 1980, 1983 and 1986
(million $US)

	Japan			USA			Canada			EC		
	1980	1983	1986	1980	1983	1986	1980	1983	1986	1980	1983	1986
China	+763	-171	+4,209	+2,591	-304	-2,135	+610	+1,096	+357	-275	+88	+2,298
Northeast Asian NICs												
South Korea	+2,353	+2,599	+5,223	+252	-1,732	-7,142	+1	-186	-579	-1,572	-849	-1,304
Taiwan	+3,180	+3,110	+3,710	-2,087	-6,687	-13,579	-211	-366	-786	n.a.	n.a.	n.a.
Hong Kong	+4,211	+4,620	+6,135	-2,341	-4,262	-6,444	-322	-486	-516	-2,265	-1,572	-1,714
ASEAN												
Indonesia	-9,754	-6,889	-4,704	-3,994	-4,191	-2,729	+112	+140	+94	+38	+929	+305
Philippines	-272	+439	-137	+86	-353	-742	+7	-9	-43	-390	-38	-512
Thailand	+800	+1,489	+644	+397	+28	-937	+98	+71	-29	-762	-356	-657
Malaysia	-1,434	-353	-2,263	-1,351	-521	-804	+11	+5	-28	-1,179	-495	-997
Singapore	+2,413	+2,981	+3,136	+1,048	+790	+1,504	+43	-31	-40	+401	+734	+627
Brunei	-3,174	-2,297	-1,243	-223	+38	+138	--	--	--	+70	+159	+168

Sources: IMF, *Direction of Trade Statistics Yearbook 1987*, tables for Japan, United States, Canada and EEC (Part A); and *Statistical Yearbook of the Republic of China 1987*, pp. 384-87.

Direct Investment

Table A-8 roughly gauges direct investment from Trilateral countries in developing East Asia. The Japanese share is the largest overall in this table (see Indonesia and South Korea in particular), and Japanese direct investment is probably increasing more rapidly than the others in the most recent period. For several particular countries, the U.S. share is the largest in the table. The European share is largest in Malaysia and Singapore.

TABLE A-8
Direct Foreign Investment in Developing East Asia, 1986
(oustanding stock at end of 1986 in million $US, and percent of total)

	Japan	USA	Europe	Others	Total
China[1]	263.4	326.2	157.0	1,497.3	2,243.7
	11.7%	14.5%	7.0%	66.7%	100.0%
South Korea[2]	2,091.3	161.0	430.3	1,373.5	4,056.1
	51.6%	4.0%	10.6%	33.9%	100.0%
Taiwan[3]	1,384.0	1,854.8	720.5	731.6	4,690.9
	29.5%	39.5%	15.4%	15.6%	100.0%
Hong Kong	513.8	1,032.0	274.1	2,272.7	2,506.0
	20.5%	41.2%	10.9%	90.7%	100.0%
Indonesia	5,251.4	1,215.8	1,863.0	7,478.6	15,808.8
	33.2%	7.7%	11.8%	47.3%	100.0%
Philippines[4]	484.0	1,671.0	407.0	530.0	3,092.0
	15.7%	54.0%	13.2%	17.1%	100.0%
Thailand	1,858.8	1,731.7	1,432.0	4,053.6	9,076.2
	20.5%	19.1%	15.8%	44.7%	100.0%
Malaysia[5]	816.0	185.6	1,007.5	960.8	2,969.9
	27.5%	6.3%	33.9%	32.4%	100.0%
Singapore[6]	1,347.3	1,710.7	1,902.4	3,384.6	5,710.0
	23.6%	30.0%	33.3%	59.3%	100.0%

Sources: JETRO, *Sekai to Nihon no Kaigai Chokusetsu Toshi* (Direct Foreign Investment of the World and Japan), 1987 and 1988; Taiwan Kenkyu-jo, *Taiwan Soran* (Taiwan Survey), 1987.

[1] flow during 1986
[2] accumulated amount, 1962-June 1987
[3] accumulated amount, 1952-86
[4] accumulated amount, 1970-86
[5] end of 1985
[6] end of 1984

ODA from Trilateral Countries

As Table A-9 indicates, in 1980 and 1986 Japan was a larger provider of official development assistance (ODA) to East Asian developing countries than Western Europe and North America combined. The EC countries together in 1986 were the largest provider of ODA to a number of individual countries: Kampuchea, Vietnam, Indonesia, Hong Kong, Taiwan and South Korea. There were net outflows from South Korea to Japan and the United States in 1986.

TABLE A-9

Total Net ODA from Trilateral Countries and Australia to East Asian Developing Countries, 1980 and 1986

(million $US)

	Japan		EC[1]		USA		Canada		Australia	
	1980	1986	1980	1986	1980	1986	1980	1986	1980	1986
China	4.3	497.0	17.2	119.7	--	--	--	18.0	0.1	14.4
Northeast Asian NICs										
South Korea	76.3	-13.7	19.3	11.1	21.0	-23.0	0.0	0.0	0.3	0.7
Taiwan	--	--	2.6	3.1	-8.0	-5.0	--	0.1	--	0.1
Hong Kong	1.1	1.6	2.2	5.1	--	--	--	0.0	0.1	7.3
ASEAN										
Indonesia	350.0	160.8	236.9	286.3	117.0	46.0	14.4	52.1	48.1	42.0
Philippines	94.4	438.0	47.4	56.8	50.0	367.0	0.2	6.1	9.8	11.6
Thailand	189.6	260.4	75.7	57.4	16.0	32.0	8.0	17.2	8.7	18.7
Malaysia	65.6	37.8	30.3	93.0	1.0	-1.0	1.0	2.5	7.3	40.8
Singapore	3.8	15.3	4.4	6.9	--	--	--	0.4	1.1	5.0
Indochina										
Vietnam	3.7	5.7	37.4	8.3	--	1.0	--	--	0.1	0.3
Kampuchea	0.1	--	32.4	1.1	--	--	--	--	4.5	1.2
Laos	1.3	5.2	2.7	1.2	--	--	--	--	0.1	3.5
Burma	152.5	244.1	57.2	39.4	--	9.0	3.7	1.1	14.4	7.0
Total	942.7	1,652.2	565.7	689.4	197.0	426.0	27.3	97.5	94.6	153.5

Sources: OECD, *Geographical Distribution of Financial Flows to Developing Countries, 1983-86* (Paris: 1988), and *Geographical Distribution of Financial Flows to Developing Countries, 1978-81* (Paris: 1983). See tables in each volume for each recipient.

[1] EC figures do not include Greece, Luxembourg, Portugal and Spain.

Participation in the IMF, World Bank and GATT

Tables A-10 and A-11 relate to the sixth point in the concluding chapter of the report (pages 52-54). They indicate that Japan's voting power in the IMF and World Bank (especially in the IMF) is low relative to the size of the Japanese economy. This is also the case for some other East Asian countries. Table A-12 relates to Chapter II (page 27). Japan, the United States, Canada, and the European Community have accepted all of the listed codes.

TABLE A-10
IMF Quotas and Voting Power
(as of 30 April 1987)

	Rank	Quota (SDR millions)	Voting Power (% of total)
United States	1.	17,918.3	19.14
United Kingdom	2.	6,194.0	6.63
FRG	3.	5,403.7	5.79
France	4.	4,482.8	4.81
Japan	*5.*	*4,223.3*	*4.53*
Saudi Arabia	6.	3,202.4	3.44
Canada	7.	2,941.0	3.16
Italy	8.	2,909.1	3.13
China	*9.*	*2,390.9*	*2.58*
Netherlands	10.	2,264.8	2.44
India	11.	2,207.7	2.38
Belgium	12.	2,080.4	2.25
Australia	13.	1,619.2	1.75
Brazil	14.	1,461.3	1.59
Venezuela	15.	1,371.5	1.49
Spain	16.	1,286.0	1.40
Mexico	17.	1,165.5	1.27
Argentina	18.	1,113.0	1.21
Sweden	19.	1,064.3	1.16
Indonesia	*20.*	*1,009.7*	*1.10*
Finland	31.	574.9	0.64
Malaysia	*32.*	*550.6*	*0.61*
South Korea	*39.*	*462.8*	*0.52*
New Zealand	40.	461.6	0.52
Philippines	*43.*	*440.4*	*0.50*
Greece	45.	399.9	0.45
Thailand	*47.*	*386.6*	*0.44*
Portugal	48.	376.6	0.43
Cameroon	86.	92.7	0.13
Singapore	*87.*	*92.4*	*0.13*

Source: IMF, *Annual Report 1987* (Washington: 1987), pp. 124-27 and 146-49.

Note: The number of votes of a country in the IMF equals its quota (in 100,000 SDRs) plus 250. The Ninth General Review of Quotas is now in process.

TABLE A-11
IBRD Shares and Voting Power

	Subscribed Shares (as of 3/31/88)		Voting Power (% of total)	Authorized Shares (as of 7/6/88)		Voting Power (% of total)
United States	1.	148,707	19.32	1.	264,969	18.19
Japan	*2.*	*40,830*	*5.33*	*2.*	*93,770*	*6.45*
FRG	3.	40,632	5.30	3.	72,399	4.98
United Kingdom	4.	38,947	5.08	4.	69,397	4.78
France	4.	38,947	5.08	4.	69,397	4.78
China	*6.*	*25,142*	*3.29*	*6.*	*44,799*	*3.09*
Saudi Arabia	7.	25,140	3.29	7.	44,795	3.09
India	8.	23,835	3.12	7.	44,795	3.09
Canada	9.	23,758	3.11	7.	44,795	3.09
Italy	10.	19,842	2.61	7.	44,795	3.09
Netherlands	11.	17,381	2.29	11.	35,503	2.45
Belgium	12.	16,266	2.14	12.	28,983	2.00
Australia	13.	13,552	1.79	14.	24,464	1.69
Brazil	14.	11,848	1.57	13.	24,946	1.73
Iran	15.	11,179	1.48	15.	23,686	1.64
Spain	16.	10,294	1.37	15.	23,686	1.64
Mexico	17.	9,553	1.27	18.	18,804	1.31
Argentina	18.	9,428	1.26	19.	17,911	1.25
Sweden	19.	8,404	1.12	21.	14,974	1.04
Indonesia	*20.*	*8,337*	*1.11*	*20.*	*14,981*	*1.04*
Venezuela	21.	7,560	1.01	17.	20,361	1.41
Malaysia	*31.*	*4,627*	*0.63*	*33.*	*8,244*	*0.58*
New Zealand	35.	4,061	0.56	38.	7,236	0.51
Philippines	*36.*	*3,841*	*0.53*	*41.*	*6,844*	*0.49*
Egypt	38.	3,619	0.50	39.	7,108	0.50
South Korea	*39.*	*3,596*	*0.50*	*29.*	*9,372*	*0.66*
Thailand	*41.*	*3,349*	*0.47*	*43.*	*6,349*	*0.45*
Portugal	42.	2,813	0.41	44.	5,460	0.39
Equatorial Guinea	124.	327	0.07	120.	715	0.07
Singapore	*125.*	*320*	*0.07*	*128.*	*570*	*0.06*

Source: World Bank

Note: The number of votes of a country in the IBRD equals its number of subscribed shares plus 250. The number of authorized shares for a country may exceed the number to which it has subscribed. The General Capital Increase (GCI) announced in early 1988 raised the authorized capital by about four-fifths. The last column in the table would represent actual voting power only if this authorized increase is fully subscribed. The recent GCI represents no change in voting shares from previously authorized levels.

TABLE A-12
Acceptance of GATT Tokyo Round Codes
(status as of 1 June 1987)

	Anti-Dumping Practices	Subsidies and Counter-vailing Duties	Govern-ment Procure-ment	Technical Barriers to Trade	Customs Valua-tion	Import Licen-sing
China			not GATT member			
South Korea	A	A		A	A*	
Taiwan			not GATT member			
Hong Kong	A	A	A	A	A	A
Singapore	A		A	A		A
Indonesia		A*				
Philippines				A		A
Thailand						
Malaysia						
Brunei[1]						

Sources: GATT, *GATT Activities 1986* (Geneva: June 1987), pp. 94-95.

Note: Acceptance of a code is indicated by "A." An asterisk indicates a reservation, condition and/or declaration.

[1] Brunei is one of those countries to which the GATT has been applied before independence and which now, as independent states, maintain a de facto application of the GATT pending final decisions as to their future commercial policy.

Political Attention

Table A-13 cannot be easily interpreted. The U.S. diplomatic presence seems to be the largest among Trilateral countries in most countries listed.

TABLE A-13
**Number of Diplomatic Representatives in East Asia
of Seven Trilateral Countries**

	France	FRG[1]	Italy[1]	UK	Japan	USA[2]	Canada
Japan	20	9	4	47	—	97	35
China	19	2	3	48	52	101	15
South Korea	8	2	3	22	41	91	11
Hong Kong	6	2	2	x	24	77	28
Indonesia	10	3	5	23	40	160	14
Philippines	10	1	2	14	31	321	16
Thailand	13	1	2	30	48	124	19
Malaysia	8	3	2	22	25	47	8
Singapore	9	1	1	22	24	53	15
Brunei	n.a.	1	1	5	8	n.a.	4
Kampuchea	n.a.	n.a.	1	0	0	n.a.	n.a.
Laos	4	1	n.a.	4	10	9	3
Vietnam	8	1	1	7	11	n.a.	3
Burma	5	1	2	11	16	38	4

Source: Masashi Nishihara, *East Asian Security and the Trilateral Countries*), p. 103.

Note: The definition of diplomatic representatives varies from country to country. The reporter has tried to include diplomats working in chanceries and press offices, as military attachés, in economic and financial departments, in scientific and cultural departments, and in consular divisions—and to exclude all other officials or quasi-officials with diplomatic status.

[1]German and Italian figures concern only ambassadors, consul generals, and consuls, excluding all other diplomatic staff. Economic and trade officers are not considered "diplomatic representation" by these countries. No other official figures are available.

[2]U.S. figures exclude federal civilian employees employed by the army, navy, air force or other military agencies in the respective countries. These figures, threrefore, represent the number of representatives from the State Department, Department of Commerce, United States Information Agency, and other civilian agencies, on December 31, 1982.

Education in Trilateral Universities

Table A-14 indicates that the United States is the Trilateral country hosting the largest· number of university students from East Asian developing countries, though the Canadian total is a little higher relative to Canada's population. The EC shows the largest rise in percentage terms (a quadrupling) between 1970 and the mid-'80s. The number of students in Japan from China and the ASEAN countries rose between 1970 and 1984, offset by fewer South Koreans.

TABLE A-14
University Students Abroad in Trilateral Countries and Australia
(unit: persons)

	Japan		EC[1]		USA		Canada		Australia	
	1970	1984	1970	1983/84	1970	1985	1970	1985	1970	1984
China[2]	3,368	5,185	479	2,078	12,324	32,400	571	1,104	51	119
Northeast Asian NICs										
South Korea	5,115	1,781	416	2,948	3,857	16,012	139	139	20	89
Hong Kong	91	124	559	5,110	9,040	9,193	2,419	7,723	1,045	1,337
ASEAN										
Indonesia	140	197	1,849	3,710	662	7,048	81	288	285	798
Philippines	55	123	81	214	2,759	3,364	104	74	58	81
Thailand	195	408	571	799	5,627	5,954	107	105	222	170
Malaysia	186	343	1,432	5,829	836	19,758	434	2,346	2,717	5,964
Singapore	52	67	417	1189	380	3,369	192	1,090	694	674
Brunei	0	1	49	771	4	29	0	42	18	21
Total	9,202	8,229	5,437	22,648	35,489	97,127	4,047	12,911	5,110	9,253

Sources: UNESCO, *Statistical Yearbook 1972* (Paris: 1973), pp. 476-80; *Statistical Yearbook 1986*, pp. 437-41; and *Statistical Yearbook 1987*, pp. 457-61.

[1] EC figures include the Federal Republic of Germany (1983), the United Kingdom (1983), France (1984), Italy (1983), Belgium (1984), and the Netherlands (1984). The 1970 figures show a concentration in the United Kingdom of students from Hong Hong (99% of total), Malaysia (96%), Singapore (96%), and Brunei (100%); and a concentration of students from South Korea (81%) and Indonesia (65%) in the FRG. The 1983/84 figures reveal similar concentration patterns.

[2] China figures refer to both Taiwan and the People's Republic of China.

APPENDIX B: INSTITUTIONAL FRAMEWORKS
FOR ASIA-PACIFIC COOPERATION

The first expressions of Japanese interest in Asia-Pacific cooperation were heard in the mid-1960s with the "Pan-Pacific Free Trade Zone Plan" advocated by Prof. Kiyoshi Kojima and the 1967 declaration by then Foreign Minister Takeo Miki on the importance of Japan's economic cooperation with the region. In the background of this sudden rise of interest in the region were increased U.S. pressure for a more active Japanese role in the international community and concern about the re-emergence of protectionism and economic blocs despite the ongoing Kennedy Round. Steady advancement of economic integration in the European Community undoubtedly also encouraged the plans for regional cooperation.

It was in this context that two of the most active Pan-Pacific institutions emerged. The Pacific Basin Economic Committee (PBEC) was established in April 1967 among businessmen from Japan, the United States, Canada, Australia and New Zealand; and this was followed by the first meeting of the Pacific Trade and Development Conference (PAFTAD) in 1969, an informal private academic group of economists from various countries in the region (the core group representing Australia, Japan, Canada, ASEAN and the United States). PBEC, now expanded to 16 country-members, has been a steady, if not the most outspoken, advocate of regional cooperation through its annual conferences and other activities. Indeed, it is noteworthy that at the 1979 PBEC annual conference a plan for a "Pacific Economic Community" was proposed. Meanwhile, PAFTAD has also met annually to promote and review policy-oriented academic studies and discussion of regional economic issues, and has become widely recognized as the major organization linking policy-oriented economists throughout the region.

The 1970s witnessed a peak in Japanese official interest in Pacific cooperation, embodied by the Pacific Basin Cooperation Concept advocated in November 1978 by the Pacific Basin Cooperation Study Group organized by then Prime Minister Masayoshi Ohira. The concept was based on three principles: (1) not to be exclusive; (2) to maintain a liberal and open system of interdependence; and (3) to mutually complement existing bilateral and multilateral relations in the region.

Prime Minister Ohira also gave birth to yet another Pacific institution. A talk between him and the Australian Prime Minister Malcolm Fraser in January 1980 resulted in the Pan-Pacific Community Seminar which later became institutionalized as the Pacific Economic Cooperation Conference (PECC). The uniqueness of the PECC, compared to the other Pacific institutions, lies in the fact that it is a group composed of government officials (who attend in a private capacity), business representatives and academics. So far six seminars have been held, in Canberra (1980), Bangkok (1982), Bali (1983), Seoul (1985), Vancouver (1986), and Osaka (1988). It is noteworthy, in light of the semi-official character of the PECC, that the Vancouver and Osaka seminars were attended by both the People's Republic of China and Taiwan as full participants and the USSR as an observer.

APPENDIX C: ORIGIN AND PURPOSES OF THE OECD

Some readers may not be familiar with the OECD, which is discussed in Chapter II in particular. This note is drawn from two principal sources. One is a book by Henry G. Aubrey entitled Atlantic Economic Cooperation: The Case of the OECD *(New York: Praeger, 1967). The other is an informational pamphlet published by the OECD itself, entitled* OECD *(Paris: September 1985).*

Membership

The OECD (Organization for Economic Cooperation and Development) was established by a convention signed in 1960 which came into force on 30 September 1961. The signatories of the convention included the 18 members of the former OEEC (Organization for European Economic Cooperation)—Austria, Belgium, Denmark, France, the Federal Republic of Germany, Greece, Iceland, Ireland, Italy, Luxembourg, the Netherlands, Norway, Portugal, Spain, Sweden, Switzerland, Turkey and the United Kingdom—plus the United States and Canada (which had been informally associated with the OEEC). Japan, in 1964, was the first Pacific country to join the OECD. In 1969, Finland became a member, followed at the beginning of the '70s by Australia and New Zealand, bringing the current total to 24 countries. The Commission of the European Communities takes part in OECD work—notably in the meetings of the Council—and Yugoslavia participates (agreement of 28 October 1961) in many activities.

Japan's admission to the OECD—its first non-Atlantic member—marked a milestone in the organization's evolution. Japan's earlier contributions to, and cooperation in, the Development Assistance Committee (DAC) foreshadowed its subsequent admission to full OECD membership, according to Aubrey.

> Nevertheless, the fact that it was sponsored by the United States implied overriding political considerations as well—the rehabilitation of a former foe, the reintegration of an important trading nation into the world economy, and the mutual accommodation of conflicting interests and divergent practices, particularly in Japan's relationships with the European OECD members....
>
> For Japan, membership in the OECD brings not only full acceptance as an industrial country but also inclusion in the group of powerful policy-makers outside the Communist bloc. It implies, moreover, the hope of full equality in trading arrangements.... (Aubrey, pp. 95-96)

At first glance, differences and disparities among member countries of the OECD may seem quite marked. "But Member countries are linked by a community of interests, common problems, a commitment to the market economy, a democratic system and—because of their combined economic weight—common responsibilities to the world at large." (OECD pamphlet, p. 5)

Origins

The OECD took over from the OEEC, which had been created in 1948 to rebuild and reconstruct the economies of Europe, with the help of $14 billion of United States Marshall Plan aid. Although the OEEC originally came into being to plan and carry out the European recovery program with American help, it later undertook to supervise the liberalization of trade.

As the OEEC countries progressed towards common economic goals, from reconstruction to self-reliance, from stabilization to economic growth, and, eventually, from restrictions to freer trade and exchanges, the organization's usefulness diminished. By the late '50s, the achievement of a large measure of convertibility among the major currencies and the elimination of many intra-European trade restrictions meant that major purposes of the OEEC had been accomplished. One part of Western Europe was already setting itself off from the rest. A tighter concept of cooperation had developed among six countries in the geographic core of Europe, which brought about the establishment of common institutions, most notably the EEC in 1957. After the breakdown of the 1958 negotiations for a Europe-wide free trade area, the "Outer Seven," comprised of Great Britain, three Scandanavian countries (Finland later became an associate member), Switzerland, Austria, and Portugal, formed the European Free Trade Association (EFTA) in 1959. This move formalized the division of Western Europe along distinct lines, and intensified the organizational crisis of the OEEC. At the same time there was a realization by the United States that Europe had changed from a beneficiary to a partner, and of the broader economic challenges and responsibilities for both in the Third World.

These factors lead to the call for a new organization broader than Europe in character. The three basic aims stated in Article 1 of the OECD Convention are:

- To achieve the highest sustainable economic growth and employment and a rising standard of living in Member countries, while maintaining financial stability, and thus contribute to the development of the world economy;
- To contribute to sound economic expansion in Member as well as non-Member countries in the process of economic development;
- To contribute to the expansion of world trade on a multilateral, non-discriminatory basis in accordance with international obligations.

Despite the demise of one institution and the creation of another, there was much more continuity than one might expect. The OEEC was an innovator of institutional procedures that the OECD inherited. Through "confrontation," consultation, and technical cooperation, OEEC Members had developed "techniques of cooperation"—initially to harmonize policies for the better use of both American aid and national resources. The procedure of confrontation, whereby each member annually submitted a statement on its economy and economic policies to the other members who scrutinized it in detail, was very useful in having an impact on policy-making in its formative stage. Aubrey writes that "[c]riticism exchanged among experts who have come to know and respect each other can be a powerful prod in the formative stages of policy-making....Confrontation is thus an informal but influential instrument of moral suasion." Equally important was the educational effect of coming to know the economy and the problems of another state, which was also helped by the OEEC publishing comprehensive, reliable and comparable economic data from every Member country.

Framework and Method

The OECD consists of several bodies: (1) the *Council*, which includes all members, is the supreme body in the OECD; the Council is under the chairmanship of the OECD Secretary-General; (2) the *Executive Committee*, a smaller body with 14 seats, prepares the business to be placed before the Council; (3) within the OECD there are more than 20 *committees plus numerous working parties and expert groups,* covering a wide range of subjects, some broad in scope, others technical and highly specialized; (4) in addition to the work that directly involves the Membership, the OECD works closely with industry and trade union *consultative bodies*— the Business and Industry Advisory Committee (BIAC) and the Trade Union Advisory Committee (TUAC); and (5) the Council, committees and other organs of the OECD are serviced by a *Secretariat* headed by a Secretary-General.

The OECD is not a supranational organization, but rather a center for discussion where governments express their points of view, share their experiences and search for common ground. As stated in its informational pamphlet, the OECD's mission is:

- To clarify, through quantitative and qualitative analyses, the economic and social problems facing its Member countries;
- To exchange information on how the problems are being approached in each country so that the experience of one can inform the actions of the others;
- To analyze the effectiveness of economic and social policies;
- Through discussion, to make countries aware of the impact of their actions on the others;
- To search for common solutions or strategies.

Agreements reached in the OECD can be embodied in more formal actions if Member countries consider it appropriate.